Kingdom
Business

Kingdom Business

The Ministry of Promoting Economic Activity

David R. Befus

Kingdom Business

© David R. Befus, 2001.
Miami, Florida, United States of America.

 Published by Latin America Mission
P.O. Box 52-7900 - Miami, FL 33152
1-800-275-8410   -   www.lam.org

Economics/Development/Social/Holistic Ministry/Missions

Printed in Colombia

First edition, August 2002.

Dedication

This book is dedicated to my father,
Clarence P. Befus
who was a missionary and businessman,
with the initiative and courage to combine
and integrate these two vocations. And to
our Lord and Savior Jesus Christ, who also
was a businessman, and knew a lot about all
kinds of productive economic activities.

SOLO DEO GLORIA.

CONTENTS

PREFACE

God called me into this ministry of economic development.

When I started as a missionary with the Latin America Mission in 1974, I had no idea that our plans for ministry with college students in Latin America would result in a service enterprise, a dormitory residence for 26 students complete with full-time cook and house administrator. This ideal context for student ministry was run as a business simply because we did not have the funds to sustain it in any other way.

I had no idea, when the Christian students in the dormitory helped start an outreach project in a slum community, that they would decide that a survey of community needs be our point of contact with the people. Nor did I know that the results of this survey would demonstrate that the greatest need was for jobs for the women, who in the majority of cases were the sole providers for the children.

When the concept of helping the women make bean bag furniture was first presented, because it was a productive economic activity they could do at home while watching the children, I had no idea that this was going to be so successful. The project changed the life of the community economically, and in the process created the foundations for a Bible study that evolved into a church.

I was so impressed by this experience that I went to the University of Michigan Graduate School of Business to study how business can be used to address the needs of the poor. My classmates were studying how to be CEOs of Fortune 500 companies, so I had no idea that I would find several professors who were very interested in helping me. One had worked with the International Labour Organization in Geneva, and assigned me several projects related to "the informal sector." Another was working on small business projects with the World Bank, and my professor of international marketing had been a missionary in Africa.

When I graduated with the MBA degree, I had no idea that there were organizations like the Institute for International Development, a Christian agency that had been started to help the poor through economic development. They hired me to organize a micro enterprise project in Honduras in 1979, the first of several I would help start through that organization, which is now called Opportunity International.

As a model for using a revolving loan program for helping the poor was developed, I became increasingly aware that, though I was teaching people how to run businesses, I had not done this myself. I had no idea how much I was going to learn from starting my own business in 1980, a physical fitness center called Gimnasio BodyArt. I learned more from operating this business than from the MBA degree, and it helped me prepare to start other small ventures both in Latin America and the U.S.

I returned to the U.S. in the 1980s to work on a doctoral degree, and to understand basic issues that I had struggled with in promoting development through business. When I started the program, I had no idea that I would also have the privilege to work in international consulting with a prestigious international company, and also see what the world looked like from the vantage point of projects with the World Bank, government agencies, and the multinational companies.

This experience and the doctoral education, with my dissertation study on international expatriate investors, was applied in jobs with World Relief and World Vision, which provided me with the opportunity to work in Africa, Asia, and Eastern Europe. I had no idea how different some of these contexts were from Latin America, and how necessary it was to contextualize methodologies to fit the environment.

Now I am back where I started, at the Latin America Mission, where business has long been an acceptable tool for the ministry of the Church. I had no idea that getting back in the Mission would also result in the opportunity to put into writing something about this journey that God has allowed me. I hope that the ideas presented in this book will result in more effective proclamation of the Gospel, and encourage Christians to communicate hope in action. May God call others, as he has called me, to the ministry of promoting productive economic activity.

Chapter 1

Business is a Ministry Tool for the Church

The witness of the church is the theme of thousands of books written by theologians and Bible scholars. Independent of that topic, in the church today there is great interest in (1) the communication of the Gospel (Jesus as Savior) in a holistic manner that gets the attention of the non-Christian, and (2) the follow-up of the evangelistic message with programs of discipleship and commitment (Jesus as Lord)to follow firmly in the faith, and (3) the financing of outreach and ministry itself, so that the testimony of the Church, the body of Christ, can be sustainable in the long term.

This book presents theory and cases of actual economic programs, entrepreneurial methodologies, and businesses that have contributed to the witness of the church. It begins with an explanation of how economic development can be used as a tool in evangelism and discipleship. Then it presents how economic tools can be used to strengthen and support projects of the church and those who are following Jesus. Some economic development programs can be utilized for both outreach and for the church congregation. One objective of the book is to present sufficient information so churches can start pilot programs to address the needs in their own community.

The book describes specific opportunities to also utilize business tools for the support of the services of church-related projects, to support ministry itself, and even to fund international mission outreach. In all of these programs, there are some management factors that are common, and some that are different. The purpose of this book is not just to present theory, but also to provide a foundation upon which to build new programs.

The last part of the book includes a presentation of the Biblical basis for these kinds of programs, and suggestions for the integration of Christian witness that are appropriate for all of the methodologies. It is hoped that these observations and ideas will be used in new programs, and also applied in existing economic development programs where the initial vision was to present the Gospel and promote Christian discipleship.

God works, and man was created in His image. Man must also work to be able to earn his daily bread. In a world with increasing levels of unemployment, it gets harder every day to find work. This book promotes a variety of methodologies to respond to this need, and explains how the promotion of productive economic activity contributes to the growth of the church, and to a presentation of a holistic Gospel that includes "doing good." It also presents concepts that the church can use to generate income to sustain it own ministries, even to the extent of funding international mission outreach.

The church needs to recognize that productive economic activity is one of many tools valuable for ministry. Economic development should be added to the "ministry toolbox," along with health, education, and other traditional ministry disciplines. The concepts presented in this book are the product of 25 years of experience of the author in promoting this idea, first in the context of evangelistic outreach with university students in Latin America, and then with three Christian development agencies in Latin America, Africa, Eastern Europe, and Asia. It makes sense. It also is possible to do.

Though many Christian non-profit organizations have programs to confront problems of unemployment and are using different methods of promoting productive economic activity for poor people, these are often isolated and disconnected with the church. There is little integration of social projects and the presentation of the Gospel. Furthermore, as many of these organizations attempt to obtain funds from government and international agencies to be able to expand their programs, we see less and less of a relationship between their development activity and the evangelistic agenda of the church. May this book help to open a door for the church, so that it can take advantage of the techniques and methodologies of economic development for the Kingdom of God.

It is important to clarify that the ideas presented in this book are not new. The history of the church is full of examples of the importance of productive economic activity:

- Apostle Paul, who utilized the mechanism of micro enterprise of leather artisan to provide for his support. We find in his first letter (I Thessalonians 2:9 "we worked night and day not to be a burden on you.") and in many other references (II Thessalonians 3:7-9; I Corinthians 9:6,18; Acts 20:34-35) we learn that Paul wanted to fund his ministry as an example for others. The reference in Acts 18 to his work "making tents" is in reference to leather working, as the tents were made out of leather.

- Religious orders such as the Franciscans and Jesuits utilized productive economic activity to finance their programs and gave a very important place to the concept of work.

- Some of the protestant denominations also used productive economic activity to support ministry and as a base for mission outreach. For example, the Moravians in 1732 sent people to India, and then to minister to the Indians in North America, with the assumption that their entire program be supported by economic activity.

- William Carey, the famous missionary pioneer, was a shoemaker, and preached that to be a missionary, it was necessary that a person have a work skill that would enable the person to sustain their needs in their chosen missionary environment.

In the last 50 years the church may have forgotten this history and examples, and now appears to be almost exclusively focused on a model that assumes the need for donations to finance ministry. The church in North America has taught this model to the rest of the world, and the formula of depending on donations is accepted everywhere. But the perception that ministry requires offerings creates great limitations for ministry. This is especially true in countries where donations are scarce. Ironically, this dependence mentality did not exist in the first century church. It is high time, therefore, to introduce again the possibility of utilizing the tools of productive economic activity and the concept of WORK as another valuable tool for Christian ministry.

As this is done, there is need to acknowledge that in some sectors of the church there is opposition to the promotion of economic development based on Christian principles. Some say that such programs are oriented towards creating wealth, which goes against the proclamation of Christian values. It should be noted that the Bible is not opposed to creating wealth, but to the love of wealth. A fact that is seldom acknowledged these days is that it is actually God, creator of universe, who gives us the ability to generate wealth. "Remember the Lord your God, for it is he who gives you the ability to produce wealth." (Deuteronomy 8:18) Not capitalism, globalism, the Internet, free markets, etc., but God. The challenge for programs that promote productive economic activity is to encourage an appropriate focus on material things without creating materialists. This is, in fact, a challenge that confronts all of us for all of our lives, independently of how much money we have.

There is great potential to involve the local church in economic development activities, and this can have many positive consequences for the church. These programs respond to the needs of non-Christians in the neighborhood. Church members may be able to get a job or increase their income. As a result, there could be an increase in support for the church through tithes. Or with a more stable financial situation, church members may have more time for church programs and activities. Furthermore, there are opportunities to create businesses that may be able to sustain church programs. Christian professionals who want to work in ministry might be able to obtain partial or full support from economic projects, or even become "tent-maker" missionaries with the ability to be involved in overseas ministry without raising financial support in their home country.

Yes. It is time to take seriously the potential of this tool- productive economic activity- and put it at the service of the Kingdom of God.

Chapter 2

Five Basic Paradigms or Models for Ministry Through Productive Economic Activity

The Centro Evangélico church in Blas de Lezo, Cartagena, Colombia is growing by leaps and bounds. Many have come to the church through its elementary school programs in the slum villages, others through the Saturday training sessions in basic business skills, and some through other programs designed to create income opportunities for the poor. The two morning services filled to overflowing and the multiple venues for evangelism and discipleship are attributed, to a large extent, to programs of outreach in economic development.

We are used to thinking of missionary doctors and teachers, but business and economics can also be a tool for Christian ministry in many contexts. Jesus taught us to pray: "give us this day our daily bread," and people want a job, not a handout. In environments like northern Colombia, where thousands are displaced by the civil war, and unemployment is over 50%, the instructions of the Apostle Paul "to make it your ambition to lead a quiet life, to mind your own business and to work with your own hands, just as we told you, so that your daily life may win the respect of outsiders and that you will not be dependent on anybody" (I Thessalonians 4:11-12) are seldom quoted. "How do we do this?" would be the question, should any preacher dare to use this as a sermon text.

Models are needed that combine economic development with a clear focus on holistic Christian outreach. They must be integrated with church ministry and a clear emphasis on Christian witness. Through the course of this book, five distinct models or paradigms of economic projects are presented for the service of the church.

The most common example, and one that is evident in the church projects in Colombia, is the service business that has the capability for generating revenue to cover its costs. These generally start out as ministry projects begun in response to a specific need for promoting health (clinics, hospitals, etc.), education (schools, literature distribution, etc.) or other ministry outreach such as camp programs and radio stations. The specific services may be initially offered for free, but a fee for service is often introduced to guarantee that the service is being valued and to help to pay for costs. Over time, as donated support deteriorates, the cost of services is generally increased, and in many cases a two-tier fee structure allows ministries to charge commercial rates to clients who are able to pay, thus allowing the ministry to subsidize services to poorer target groups.

Ministry Service Businesses

...the development of self-sustaining enterprises such as Christian clinics, dental offices, schools, and bookstores, where the ministry charges a fee for services. Some of these projects, like the Clínica Bíblica (hospital) in Costa Rica, have grown to have multi-million dollar budgets. The Colegio Latinoamericano in Cartagena, Colombia (elementary and high school) has over 800 students. Both of these projects were initiated by missionaries, developed national leadership, and have been run for several decades by national boards recruited from local church leadership.

Another type of economic enterprise that has evolved in relation to overseas ministry is the ministry endowment enterprise, commercial activity that is developed solely for the financial support of local ministry. The concept of "endowment" is quite popular in Western Christian institutions, a contemporary cornerstone of the financing of most Christian colleges and seminaries. Overseas institutions also struggle with the need to create a long-range foundation for financial sustainability, facing fewer opportunities for local self-support due to a poorer national population, and also confronting donor fatigue. In this context many overseas ministries have created innovative businesses organized solely to generate funds for ministry, managed as completely separate units.

Ministry Endowment Enterprises

...for a local foundation for long-term support of Christian ministry in the field. For example, the Granja Roblealto, an agricultural farm that produces chickens and pigs in Costa Rica, employs more than 90 people, but was created to support the children's ministries. It channeled over $200,000 in direct financial support to local Christian day care centers and other children's ministries in 1999. Scripture Union of Lima, Peru operates a fleet of taxis that employ people and fund a major portion of their ministry costs. Entrepreneurial missionaries and donors began both of these projects.

Related to the "endowment" approach is the use of "tent-making" enterprise to support ministry for the mobilization of missionaries from Latin America to the rest of the world. The local church in Latin America is generally not able to fund the full cost of expatriate ministry overseas. Innovative international business concepts are being developed to allow Latin American missionaries not only to generate a substantial portion of their costs from business activity, but also to secure visa permits. These "tent-making" operations require business concepts that exhibit a comparative advantage in technology or markets that result in a viable and profitable enterprise, and are not just a "platform" to get into a country. An added benefit of this enterprise activity is that is creates a social context to meet and minister to local people that is often more understandable than "full-time Christian worker."

Tent-Making Enterprises

...to provide legal entry, financial support, and a ministry context for expatriates. A Mexican family is able to minister in a Muslim country because they set up a retail store, which provides the major part of their monthly income, as well a context for ministry. Another group in Mexico is sending out people with training in specialized ceramics, and in the restaurant business. In all of these cases the initial business concepts, loan funding for the projects, technology, product supplies, and overseas connections involved expatriate missionary consultants.

The church in the developing world is increasingly confronted by the poverty that surrounds it, as economic globalization has resulted in declining levels of income for the poor majority. Responding to this situation, many ministry programs have added job creation to the traditional missionary outreach of health and education. The business incubator development approach is being used in many mission contexts to increase income levels and generate employment for church members, and as an evangelistic tool targeted at specific populations. The business incubator promotes viable business projects to create employment or generate income.

Business Incubators

...the creation of new businesses for target populations needing income or employment, but not having a background or experience in productive economic activity. The ministry generates the business idea and the ministry controls all assets until the participants have learned to make products on their own. For example, street teenagers from a youth center in Mexico (street children turn into street teenagers!) are taught how to make puppets and stuffed animals. Through business activity, these young people learn to support themselves and stay off the street. As they are able, the production activity is transferred to their homes, the equipment provided is paid back, and these funds are used for new enterprises. An entrepreneurial missionary started this.

Another increasingly popular approach to helping poor people in developing countries is micro credit programs. These require the development of sustainable revolving loan credit programs for people who have business experience and the capacity to manage a loan. The reason that many mission organizations are interested in developing these projects, rather than relying on existing specialist agencies that do such work, is that the poor populations served by the church are generally not eligible for assistance from any other source. Furthermore, many existing Christian organizations that offer programs in the area of micro credit shun integration with church programs overseas, for fear that any direct involvement with church programs might adversely affect their rate of return. At the same time, the interest rates that these agencies offer are often considered too high.

Many church-based models have been created to do micro credit on a small scale that also allows for close ties to church and ministry outreach. The success of these models is seen not only in rates of return and sustainability of the projects, but also in the economic benefits to those in the church, and the outreach opportunities for those who do not know the Gospel. Involvement in helping a person with their business allows for direct contact on an intensive level, and many opportunities for witness.

Micro Credit Programs

> ...revolving loan programs for people who have a business idea, and usually some experience, and who, with an additional capital, can generate funds to pay back the loan with interest. It generally requires an administrative unit capable of organizing basic paperwork, evaluating loan proposals, disbursing loans, providing training, collecting loans, and financial reporting. The OPDS program in Barranquilla, Colombia, is an LAM affiliate ministry with assignment of one LAM missionary family. It operates a small loans program averaging $350/family to allow poor people to begin to fully support their families, and many of these are displaced people from the civil war in Colombia. The economic programs are integrated with church outreach of the AIEC denomination.

The economic development program of the Centro Evangelistic Church was started after unsuccessful attempts to get help from other Christian organizations. Many have tried to promote programs related to economic development with Christian non-profit organizations that specialize in this area, but have found that their prospective "clients" do not qualify for loans or assistance. It may be that the prospective beneficiaries are not in the right geographic area or do not have sufficient experience or collateral. The phenomenon of "mission creep" seems to take place very quickly in business projects, where integration with the church and focus on the poor can quickly disappear. For whatever reason, outsourcing such programs is often not an alternative, and the church needs to develop the capacity to implement such programs themselves.

This is why the potential of economic development and job creation programs is described in this book. Like programs in health and education, the economic development tools are great resources for ministry outreach, ever more relevant in a world where poverty and unemployment are rampant. The next section of the book explores the first steps in applying these specific models in the church.

Chapter 3

The Church Community and the Promotion of Productive Economic Activity

As the case is presented for the promotion of economic activity as an integral part of the ministry of the church, it is necessary to first address certain assumptions about the relationship between these types of projects and the church. God created work to provide for man's daily bread, and people in and outside the church often need work and increased income. The daily activity of a person in the job environment also provides a great social context to get to know them, and an excellent opportunity for evangelism and discipleship. In the workplace you can see how they treat others, how they handle money, how they react to stress... you can see how they really live.

It is for this same reason, in successful programs that are integrated with the church, that it is necessary to separate the administration of these projects from the church itself. Such a separation has three specific benefits for the "clients" of the project:

- The system for service delivery must be allowed to promote ONLY sustainable activity, and also become sustainable itself based on some type of revenue generated through its services. For this to function, it requires an administration and operation independent of the church.
- A critical aspect of this is that only financially viable projects be funded, i.e. only economic activity that makes a profit. The determination of viability in the real world market requires independence in decision-making, and specifically the ability to say "no" to proposals that do not demonstrate economic viability, regardless of who presented them.
- The funds generated by successful projects can be recycled and used over and over again, thereby multiplying the benefits for those in need at no cost whatsoever. This will work only if the funds are separated from church funds, with an accounting that is restricted for economic development projects.

The purpose is to generate income and create employment, within or outside the church, through viable projects that allow for the recycling of resources. Productive activity that is profitable in the real world market place can be funded only after a careful investigation, and it must show a return that can either pay back the investment or allow funds to be used by others. The idea is to promote a resource that will maintain or increase its value, even while helping others.

True economic development is a ministry tool based on viable projects, not handouts or donations. The discipline required to enable a business to be profitable in the competitive marketplace is the same faced by any other commercial business. Unprofitable economic activity, in the Christian ministry sector, is quite sad, because instead of generating revenue, it consumes donations that often are intended for other types of programs. Traditional church-funded businesses, like sewing projects for groups of women, have a history of subsidized production generating poor quality products that are not marketable. Such "photo-opportunity" projects are NOT what are desirable, as they also tend to create another experience of failure for those involved.

This is why the separation of the economic projects from the church is also good for the church ministry. Not all of the needy people that the church wants to help will be interested or willing to get involved in serious, disciplined economic activity. A separate organizational unit managing this project can make determinations about involvement and participation that will not affect relationships in the on going church ministry.

It sometimes also happens that church people do not act with integrity, and this is quickly discovered in a business environment. To identify this problem may be of benefit to the life and Christian walk of that person, but to confront it may be difficult or destructive in the church environment.

There are three important principal actors that are key to good management of economic development projects that are integrated with, but managed separately from, the church:

1- **The operational entity.** An organization that often begins as a small committee, and then may evolve into a legal association with a board, operational procedures, its own accounting system, personnel, and assets.

The monitoring of invested capital or loans is often made much easier by an operational unit or board that is separate from the traditional programs of the church, as the perception of the church is sometimes as a "voluntary organization that collects funds, and does not need me to pay." Sometimes people also get confused by a vision of the church as "my church, so this is really my (our) money, so why should I pay for anything?" The establishment of a separate entity to handle economic or business programs also reduces legal risk that the church might incur.

> **2- The church.** Provides the supervision needed during the start-up phase, and then participates through members who are on the board, as the project matures.

The ideas that the program is operationally separate means that the church must work hard to integrate the project with the ministry of the church. The opportunities for direct and indirect Christian witness should be central to the church's view of the program. Later in this book the basic Biblical fundamentals and concepts are presented to help implement programs of outreach. This is also a project that lends itself to serious discipleship, as the participants are involved in an environment where one can deal with far more than their Sunday best, and see, up close and personal, how they behave in the real world.

The church also participates through the placement of leaders on the organizational committee. The initial recruiting of a board should be in mind even as the project is conceived. The relationship of the economic programs to the church should also be established by written definition. This might include the condition that board membership, at least a certain number, be reserved for people from the church or churches involved in project start-up. There also might be informal agreements related to devotional participation, assistance with training programs, project visitation, etc. From the start there needs to be a commitment to a permanent relationship between the church and the organization it creates, maybe through a leadership group that will be able and willing to coordinate technical assistance and help with matters like fund raising.

> **3- The funders.** They not only provide the resources, but also participate personally in oversight, receiving regular reports, providing technical and administrative assistance, and assuming a role based on their particular background of experience. Sometimes they are closely involved, staying in close communication and visiting the projects, and sometimes they are not.

The provision of funding must balance the need for initial capital inputs with a plan to promote sustainability over time. Too much money will create dependence, and not enough will starve the program. Funders therefore play a significant role not only through providing resources, but also by reducing external support. After all, productive economic activity should be able to fund itself. How this happen is described in the next chapter.

Chapter 4

First Steps in Organizing the Project

The promotion of productive economic activity, independent of methodology, should always begin with an emphasis on the target group, or the "clients." A study should be done of the needs of the potential clients. This should also include interviews with other organizations offering the same services, to evaluate other points of view about what the critical needs are and how they can be addressed or satisfied. The purpose of this research is not just to arrive at a clear definition of the target group, but also to promote positive relationships with other organizations that might also be trying to help, and whose programs might be complementary.

In some cases it might be a good idea to simply work with others rather than create a new economic development program. For example, in a project of an association of churches in Ciudad Bolivar in Santa Fe de Bogotá, Colombia that promotes a loan program for funding productive activities, an arrangement was crafted with an existing development agency that was already working in that community. This presented other opportunities for Christian witness with this partner organization as well. However, the focus and orientation of the church often is very different from that of other organizations, so this kind of cooperation does not always work in practice.

There are several basic principles also to consider before starting a program:

> • *The program should be seen as a means to ministry, and not as an end in itself.* The key objective of the church is evangelism and discipleship. What is seen in many programs is that this objective can be lost, and the considerable work of promoting economic activity becomes just another social program, or in the worst case, another commercial business. There are many Christian schools and hospitals that started as strategic ministries of the church, and today are completely secular institutions. They are sustainable, often profitable, and may even help the poor, but they have lost the principal vision for which they were created.

The same phenomenon has taken place in many micro credit programs, some of which were created quite recently by Christian organizations. In a period of less than 20 years these have essentially lost all connection with the church. Some of them still have promotional information that they use in English fund-raising materials that point to Christian foundations or background, but in their field programs they minimize any contact with the church "to promote a better collection performance" or to placate government and institutional donors. It is interesting how quickly this phenomenon of "mission creep" can happen.

Maybe the biggest surprise are organizations started to help the poor as a Christian witness strategy, which today have evolved into big businesses, or into service organizations focused only on the wealthy. A model project in micro finance that was created to replace the market moneylenders becomes, itself, a very high interest moneylender. A school designed to help the poor and disadvantaged becomes the school for the upper class. A clinic that began as a program for the indigent is now focused only on treatment for the wealthy. Such cases exist in many places, and serve to remind us of the danger of losing the vision, and also the need to begin with a focus on the targeted beneficiaries of the program. The well-being of the organization offering the services can easily become a higher priority than the well-being of the people it was created to help, and the main focus of management turns inward. The institutionalization of the program is important as a basis for serving others, not for serving the institution and its employees.

- *It is necessary to plan from the very beginning for a sustainable or viable project, which also requires a sustainable service system.* The success of economic programs is perhaps more visible than other types of projects because they depend on having a viable project design. When programs offer services that are subsidized, it is often hard to tell whether the projects are really effective. People are generally happy to receive the product or services for free, even if it is of poor quality or not really necessary. When subsidies are depleted, such projects simply disappear.

The operational design of economic projects has to be viable. If local people cannot pay for curative medicine available when missionary doctors work at no cost, it is unlikely that paid local doctors are a viable alternative, and perhaps the medical objectives need to be met through less expensive, more transferable preventive approaches. If local people cannot pay for private schooling available when volunteer teachers work at no cost, it is unlikely that paid local teachers are a viable alternative, and perhaps the school will have to either shift its ministry focus to a mix of lower and middle-class families, or change its educational delivery (two shifts per day, larger classes, etc.) to be viable in the long run. These are the types of questions that need to be considered from the very beginning of starting a project.

What this means for projects designed to create employment is even more serious, because technical review of proposed investments in projects will be necessary to determine whether the projects can succeed. It is frequently easier to make a better margin selling products than to produce them, but many people may know more about production than sales. Through qualified technical staff assigned to the project, it may be necessary to learn a lot about potential markets before financing projects, with the goal of obtaining a higher margin and better profits for producers. This type of concern has led many organizations that work in economic development to create marketing cooperatives, identify export markets, and recommend to new business entrepreneurs only strategies that allow for sufficient product differentiation to obtain sufficient profit margins.

The world marketplace is becoming increasingly competitive, and this affects small business as well as big business. The small businessperson is at a disadvantage because he or she may not have the technology or market knowledge. For this reason it is important that information be provided to help the small company compete with quality products. The assistance of consultants from the U.S. business community, short term or long term, can play an important role in promoting innovation, attractive product design, and alternative markets. Another way to help improve margins is to cut costs. Within the church community there is tremendous potential for Christians who have businesses to work together in both collective purchasing and assistance with marketing.

It is generally these types of competitive considerations that make the business incubators work: a special market, a proprietary technology, etc. These factors are often more important in the success of a project, than the financing of the endeavor. The assumption is that programs of economic development will be viable in the real world marketplace, and that is not an easy task. Donors who provide capital for economic projects without questioning the viability of the business model may actually have a negative impact on the outcome of the funded project.

- *The program should not represent a burden for the church.* This is another reason to separate these projects organizationally and financially through the creation of a specialized operational entity. For all of the economic development programs, the goals of financial sustainability must be balanced with other objectives, and this is a tough balancing act. One may desire to charge very little for health care, schooling, or the use of financial resources. However, the fees must cover costs, or the "rental fee" on financial assets (i.e. interest) or profit margin must be sufficient to cover the costs of services provided, offset deflation/devaluation, and provide a reserve for bad debts. Special services like training may need to be funded with specific fees, and any legal or registration costs also must be taken into account.

- *There must be adequate financial systems and internal controls.* The task of creating economic enterprises as a ministry has all of the complications of the world of commerce and banking, but a professional foundation of volunteers and leaders from the local congregation. This is a great challenge! For many lay people, these types of projects are a source of great blessing, because they find in them a way to use their professional skills in Kingdom activity. It is often the case, however, that the human resources for oversight of these programs are few, and it may even be necessary to look for help from other churches or organizations.

Whatever the capacity of the leadership committee, with economic projects it is necessary to define, from the very beginning, the financial system and controls for accounting, to guarantee a proper functioning of the program. These are projects that involve investment of money, and there can be temptations to take advantage of this for personal benefit. Though separate from the church operationally, these projects do impact on the testimony of the church, and should therefore be done "in an orderly and fitting way." (I Corinthians 14:40)

- *Reporting and evaluations are required of all programs.* Monitoring of the project through monthly reports is very important, and should include both financial and social information. All members of the organizing committee should read and evaluate these reports, and the leadership of the program should also share them with the church leadership. In cases where donors are involved, they will also need to receive periodic reports.

For the project to be operational, basic definitions of reports are required. The form of reporting depends on the methodology of the project, but usually includes basic financial performance information, reports on what management and staff did during the period, identification of special problem issues that may require board awareness and participation, and descriptive information about project impact. It is very important that information on changed lives be presented in reporting, to help maintain the vision for which the program was created.

It is also a good idea to plan for evaluations that compare the initial plan to the actual outcomes. For evaluation as well, the presentation of financial reports is important to measure some very important goals, but not all of them. For this reason, other information needs to be presented in the evaluation. How does the scale of the project, in terms of numbers of people impacted, compare with expectations? How does the efficiency of the services, for example, the time between a request for a loan and its disbursement, compare to other organizations? What has been the impact of the project on the people it was designed to serve? Perhaps they are the ones most important in evaluating the success of the program.

Reporting is greatly facilitated by computerized systems, which help not only with financial records, but also in keeping a database of information on the clients of the program. Economic ministry projects that are successful quickly develop a capacity to handle reporting with computers. Especially in micro enterprise programs, it is almost impossible to keep track of loans, payments, and client information without a microcomputer. As the organization grows, or if there is substantial outside funding, it is also often necessary to contract external auditors to report on an annual basis.

The evolution of an economic development project usually follows a growth pattern along these lines:

a) **Identify and organize the start-up committee.** Recruit the initial leadership group from people in the church that can implement the vision over time.

b) **Initial investigation of the target group.** Begin to identify potential clients, analyze their needs, potential, resources, and the environment in which they live.

c) **Recruit volunteer staff.** Volunteers are needed at the beginning to help with the project organization, and generally are people with potential to become employees, who could promote an efficient administration of the program and who have a vision for the project.

d) **Further develop the vision.** Define the specific nature of the program, goals, objectives, and policies. Begin to develop and circulate a written draft of the plan for the project. Also begin to define basic policies and procedures for operation. Since projects are often born in the church, it may be useful to start with the church's written policy and procedures manual, and develop additional statements relevant to the project being organized. It is especially important to define, from the beginning, all necessary controls dealing with how money is handled.

e) **Select the director.** Choose a person who will be responsible for managing the project. This should be done with input from the church, and participation of members of the committee, which will also grow into a first board of directors for the project.

Economic ministry programs often start within the church with a group of volunteers. As the project takes shape and volunteers can no longer do the work, a full-time employee is often chosen, supervised by the church committee who can assume the overall responsibility for the program. This person coordinates the work of volunteers, and is responsible for reports and the development of the organization phase of the project. As the project takes on its own identity, the director also becomes involved in the contracting of other personnel, as well as overseeing the drafts of the plan, budget, policies, and related forms.

f) **Begin with government registrations.** In most cases the project will require a special legal status, depending on the laws governing the particular project. Sometimes churches begin economic projects, and even schools and clinics, without getting government approval, and this can have very unfortunate consequences. The Biblical principal of "submitting to authority" (I Peter 2:13) applies, as the project should also be a testimony to society of good work, and work done well.

g) **Write a strategic plan outline.** In many cases the initial idea has been developed with creative thinking, input from external donors, and reference to other organizations. All of this must now be put in the context of the research and findings from steps a-f, and a pilot plan for 3-5 years defined in writing, that includes not only a definition of service delivery methods, but also a financial analysis of project sustainability.

h) **Define the basic policies.** Depending on the local conditions and analysis of the clients, write out the initial operational policies, including reporting expectation. This may also require the cooperation of the church, as well as members of the board. The policy definitions should also include the forms that are proposed for analysis of projects, presentation of business plans, documentation for authorization of investments, oversight of field staff, etc.

i) **Define the services.** Having evaluated the needs of the target group, a program is designed based on the local environment, and taking into account available resources, and also sustainability targets.

j) **Define the geographical focus.** It is often important to limit initial services to a specific area, generally where the church is located or where it is involved in other projects, as there are limited resources available.

k) **Recruit and contract personnel.** If some have been working as volunteers on the start-up of the project, they may have already proved themselves for possible full-time employment in the project. Often the first opportunity is given to church members, though it is very important to make sure that selection is based on qualifications, not church membership.

In some cases, economic ministry requires specialized personnel due to the nature of the project being funded. For example, the start-up of a clinic requires people with medical backgrounds; a school requires educators, etc.

In the case of economic development ministry, initial staffing involve project supervisors who can introduce the program to potential clients, visit existing projects and provide technical assistance, offer business training, and use formal and informal opportunities to be a witness for Christ. The field supervisor is key to the success of economic ministry, both in terms of financial goals and ministry goals.

l) **Design the information system.** The accounting and financial controls are important to define before the project grows very large, and when possible a computer system should be used to reduce costs.

An interesting aspect of the process of institutional development is that the people who are involved in the initial start-up are not able, in many cases, to manage the project as it grows. As the project grows, the capacity of the director and staff should be evaluated periodically, and it should be expected that changes may be needed. Also at the level of the organizing committee and board, there may be the need to recruit new people, even from outside the church circle of contacts, resulting in lower levels of control in exchange for higher levels of professionalism. The difficulty in "letting the project loose" as it grows is similar, in some ways, to parents who begin to let their children go as they mature. This is a positive development, but not always easy.

The organizational committee, drawn initially from the church, develops into a full board of directors. The need for a board usually comes up when the legal registrations are investigated, and the names that are on the first legal documents may all be of people in the church. As the organization becomes operational, it will become apparent who is really interested and able to function on the board. The board is often important not only for oversight, but as a condition for obtaining funds and support from other organizations.

The principal role of the board is to supervise the director. It is not desirable that the board get involved in the daily operations or administration of the programs, but rather that it receive reports, participate and approve plans, and evaluate results. There is a natural tension between a director and the board, because all of the authority of the program resides in the board, whereas the daily responsibility lies with the director. The fact that board members are voluntary adds to this tension, as the occasional involvement of board members can be viewed by full-time staff as lack of commitment, when it actually may be simply lack of time. There are at least six areas where the board should invest the time it does have to supervise the program:

1. *Maintain the vision for the program.* This includes not only the Christian nature of the organization, but also the desire to balance the goal of financial sustainability with addressing the needs of the target group.
2. *Supervision of the finances.* This includes the review and approval of the annual plan and budget, the monthly review of reports, and an evaluation at year's end. It is also a good idea, in the case of loan projects, that one board member be a part of the committee that approves the loans.
3. *Promote the program with others.* Usually it is expected that every board member be a donor, or bring other donors into the program. They also represent the organization with other organizations, the local business community, and the local churches.
4. *Provide specialized technical assistance.* An important incentive for many board members is the opportunity to use their own skill and experience in consulting activity targeted either at the program management or at the businesses that it operates or funds.
5. *Legal representation of the organization.* The legal charter generally designates the board members as the official representatives from the perspective of the government.
6. *Pastoral oversight of the director.* This includes an interest in his/her daily well-being as a person, and not only in relation to the performance and progress of the project.

The director also needs to understand and accept that the promotion of the participation of board members is one of his/her jobs, and a legitimate and necessary use of time. The director should be willing to seek out the advice of board members on specific issues, adjust work plans to adapt to schedules of board members, and organize meetings at an hour and a place that maximizes board member participation. It is very important for the director to remember that participation in the board is voluntary, whereas all of the others involved are getting paid for their time.

So the project begins to function first as a committee of the church. Then, as it grows, it becomes a separate legal entity, developing as an organization with its own staff, management, and board of directors. At full maturity, the relationship with the church continues, even though all board members and staff may not participate in the particular church that began the project. The initial vision is kept in focus, and the connection with the initiating church also is maintained-it is part of the family, no matter how big it grows.

Chapter 5

Cost Coverage
Service Enterprises

The most common business activity promoted by the church is the service enterprise, and often these projects begin without any plan to operate a business. There are also many cases where churches are operating service enterprises without acknowledging that they are, in fact, using a business model for ministry. Given the present scarcity of funding for subsidized projects, the service business is also one of the most popular approaches for promoting sustainable ministry outreach.

The genesis of the service enterprise is usually a ministry that covers some of its own costs through service fees, but which often starts as a subsidized venture. The most common projects that come out of the church are schools and clinics, which often are born within the church premises. Camp programs, bookstores, and radio and television stations are also often begun as church ministries. The need to cover costs often develops over time, when a major donor pulls out, or when costs grow beyond the capability of the local congregation to subsidize them. Sometimes the recognition that a business model will need to be applied comes in the context of severe budgeting problems. Foreign missions sometime abandon overseas projects that they can no longer sustain, claiming this as a "nationalization" process, and motivating a speedy reorganization of the project with a business model. Whatever the origin, service enterprises find themselves in an environment where cost coverage is required for survival.

A first characteristic of a ministry service enterprise is the need to balance the objective of survival with the objectives of ministry. For example, if a clinic was started to reach out to the needs of the poor, and can no longer be sustained with donations, how can the objective of serving the poor be combined with the need to collect enough funds to operate? Or if a school was started to provide Christian education to church members, but most church members cannot afford to pay tuition, how will the school be able to continue?

What this balancing of objectives requires is an evaluation of a combination of approaches that allows for economic survival without sacrificing other objectives. These approaches include:

a) **The full costing strategy.** A careful evaluation of the total costs which are passed on to clients through fees, minus any donations, offerings, or subsidies that can be obtained.

b) **The "Robin Hood" strategy.** A widening of the target group to include people who can pay higher fees, and thus offset the cost of those paying lower fees. A health clinic might have a special program for more wealthy clients, not because they are part of the target group, but rather because they are charged a good deal more than others. A school might recruit a wide range of pupils from different economic backgrounds, and highly subsidize poorer families through a scholarship program funded by those paying full fees.

c) **The synergy, related services strategy.** Many ministries have facilities and assets that can generate revenue when not being used in ministry. For example, a camp that is used intensively for church ministry during weekends and summer rents out its facilities to businesses and schools for contracted conferences during the week and school year. Another camp center has created a program for housing an overseas studies program during its off-season.

The struggle with cost recovery may also result in substantial reorganization of the ministry. For example, many Christian bookstores have given up expensive retail space and refocused their "business model" on the placement of Christian books in existing retail establishments. The Christian literature is still being made available, but in a different manner.

In cases like this, the project may have been started with a subsidy because the target group was not able to cover the real costs. As the subsidy evaporated from donor fatigue, and the ministry had to look for a way to survive, the target group may also have changed. For example, the type of person who buys Christian books at a grocery store is probably quite different from the person who makes a special trip to the Christian bookstore. As service enterprises change their delivery system, they also need to reflect on how this is impacting their target group, and how it affects their initial goals and objectives.

The separation of these projects from the church is important, in part because of this phenomenon of needing to evolve and adjust. For example, when a school that was started within a church grows to a certain level, it generally needs to demonstrate both quality in teaching and the ability to cover its costs. Often the church exerts pressure contrary to these–promoting the hiring of church members without sufficient regard for their teaching qualifications, and expecting special prices for children of church members or church attendees. The perception of benefits to the church can result in the total destruction of the project.

The administration of service projects is made easier by the existence of operating guides and manuals, and also professional associations of all kinds. Many resources are available from academic sources, libraries, the Internet, etc. Two issues, which are critical and perhaps not addressed in many other places, are (1) the importance of setting prices, and (2) the integration of service enterprise with Christian ministry.

The decision of how to set prices is the most critical to both ministry and economic survival, and should be reviewed by the management, board, and church leadership of ministry service projects. The prices should generally be set at the level of cost coverage, not to generate a profit. But this begins to get complicated, because costs include salaries of employees, the ability to spend money on new plant and equipment, etc. Spending on these items may be of benefit to management, so management should not make these decisions alone. Furthermore, the costs may vary greatly with the anticipated scholarships for those who cannot pay full costs, and this also needs careful supervision. The definition of costs is also impacted by the definition of quality of services. For example, if a school packs 40 students in a classroom, it will need a lot less revenue per student than if class size is held to 25, but also will sacrifice quality of instruction. One additional factor added to the cost equation is funding for future project expansion, another area in which the board needs to be involved.

The issue of integration with ministry is especially important for service businesses, because they usually have the promotion of Christian witness as a key objective. Given the fact that there may be tension between a maturing project and the church that helped to start it, due to the inability to hire more employees from the church or provide lower prices to church members, the evaluation of integration is made more complex. What often occurs is a move from denominational focus to interdenominational, a natural result of the need to find both qualified employees and sufficient clients for a sustainable operation. Strong leadership with a vision for ministry is especially critical in this context, to embrace the Christian vision of the project even as its outreach expands beyond the initial group that started it.

The service enterprise approach is one in which the enterprise itself is expected to yield opportunities for Christian testimony. This purpose is completely impossible if:

- The teacher is mean and unfair with the students.
- The doctor treats the patient coldly and cares little about his/her health.
- The camp counselor acts in an immature and improper manner.

What is apparent is that this approach requires intensive training of the staff and constant reflection on how the project is communicating the Good News.

It is also necessary periodically to evaluate how the project is relating to the church and Christian ministry, and to promote renewal of a vision for integration of the project with the local church.

Chapter 6

Businesses for Sustaining Ministry: Endowment and Tent-Making

The concept of generating financial support from sources besides donations and fees has long been accepted in funding of Christian higher education. Bible schools, Christian colleges, and seminaries often derive a major portion of their annual budget from funds that are invested in the stock market or in other fixed investments, and listed in their financial statements as endowments.

In contexts where financial markets are unstable, the idea of endowment funding cannot be based on passive investments, and therefore requires a rethinking of the term "endowment." If business activity can be identified that will help generate a stable cash flow for ministry, and there are donors who are willing to invest in such businesses, this can be a very positive means of support for Christian outreach. From a field perspective, it is necessary to consider the importance of such support for many types of ministries where services cannot generate fees, and where the future of the program is dependent on donated funds. The consideration of stable support foundations for ministry is a sign of leadership maturity, and the need to plan for the longer term.

For projects initially funded from overseas, the critical need for consideration of stable support foundations is also evidence of a lapse in planning by many foreign organizations that started overseas projects with donations. It is interesting that not even in Bible seminaries was consideration of endowment support part of "nationalization plans" for such projects, ignoring the fact that without such support in North America, many of these seminaries would cease to exist. The irony is that many seminaries in developing countries struggle to survive with less capacity to charge students, and no endowment support whatsoever.

The interest in the concept of endowment funding is also the result of donor fatigue and the realization that long-run programs cannot be supported with short-term donations. Many causes, and even regions of the world, seem to be fads that change over time. Donors also age, and the favorite causes of younger people in the church are quite different from the older generation. Yet there are many projects–street children ministry, prison ministries, rehabilitation of drug addicts, etc.—that will never be able to generate fees for their support. A subsidy is needed, and if donors do not want to be involved, where else can it come from?

God is raising Christian professionals with backgrounds in business to respond to this question. Groups are being formed to develop businesses for the financial support of a variety of ministries. The objectives of these support groups go beyond fund raising, as this context provides a significant opportunity for interaction for professionals, and also many contexts for overseas ministry. For example, in the business plan for financial support of a seminary in South America, there is a description of the English classes that will take place in the seminary building during hours when classrooms are not being used in pastoral training. But there is also a plan for evangelism and discipleship of the professional people who are enrolled in the English classes.

The idea that business projects can be used to support ministry is also good for ministry. For example, in the chicken farm mentioned previously, where an agricultural project helps to provide income for a children's ministry, one of the benefits is that even the children can see that their support comes from hard work. The farm is located adjacent to housing where 70 children live, and many of the spouses of project staff also work at the farm. The children also consume eggs and chickens that cannot be sold on the market; they know where much of their food comes from. Resources generated by productive economic activity produce an ethos different, and more positive, from resources from donations.

There is a growing recognition in the church of this alternative, and many new projects being designed. The projects tend to be fairly large and more complex, requiring technical assistance from people with experience in making business plans and seeking venture capital. There are at least two Christian venture capital firms already funding such projects, and also several U.S. Christian business network organizations offering to help with technical assistance.

Much of the technical assistance available from U.S. organizations for starting a business with Christians is targeted specifically at business creation used as a missionary strategy. One factor that motivates this model of ministry business is the desire to promote Christian outreach in countries where a business is an acceptable means of entry for Christians with an interest in evangelism, but full-time missionaries are not welcome. Another important factor, especially for people in developing countries that desire to participate in foreign missions outreach, is simply the opportunity to generate an income. This was the strategy used by the Apostle Paul years ago, who throughout his ministry worked to support himself, to be an example for others. (I Corinthians 9, II Thessalonians 3)

The idea of using business as a "platform" is based on the fact that a business investment allows expatriate personnel to obtain visas, and within the daily business environment, have an understandable social context in which to meet local people. However, it is critical that the people involved in this type of activity have legitimate business activity, and are not just availing themselves of a disguise to get into a specific country. Business as a cover for full-time mission work is a deception that will, in the long run, limit and restrict genuine economic ministry projects.

The strategy of starting a business overseas is also quite different from personal tent-making, which usually refers to an individual who is able to obtain a placement in the foreign job environment. Such a job also helps with the visa, but often the secular workplace does not allow much time for overt Christian witness. Some overseas jobs specifically restrict contact with nationals. The lifestyle of the comparatively wealthy expatriate professional also creates a barrier to relationships with the local church, and also great temptations to pursue personal career path objectives, rather than to spend time in ministry. The creation of a local business bypasses many of these problems, and is more amenable to ministry opportunities.

The example of Paul is a good case for thinking about missionary businesses. He worked to generate his salary, and was a sole proprietor, who had full control of his business. His vocation as a leather artisan was apparently highly paid throughout the Roman Empire, and his business was sufficiently profitable that a single person needed to work only a few days per week to support himself, leaving the other days free for ministry activity. (Acts 18: 1-4)

The key for this economic ministry is to find the right business that permits such freedom: sufficiently profitable to generate a continual income, and sufficiently flexible to allow sufficient time for ministry. At the local level, for many pastors in the developing world, the small corner store, often operating out of a room in their house, has served as an additional source of income to sustain the ministry. For missionaries going overseas, perhaps the current equivalent to leather tent production might be computer consulting. Successful ministry businesses include restaurants, solar energy promotion, ceramics production, educational supplies and services, computer supplies and services, business consulting services, product sales representatives, and many others.

Creativity and innovation are necessary when designing profitable overseas businesses that can be set up with limited investment funds, that do not require advanced degrees, and that can, at the same time, demonstrate a competitive advantage that results in an acceptable profit margin. Oftentimes a background and experience in business is necessary for a person to be successful with an international business enterprise. Though the first mission business was organized by the first church missionary over 2000 years ago, this is an area on the pioneer fringe of church mission work today.

Chapter 7

Economic Programs Focused on Helping the Poor

The three previous models of using economic tools for ministry were focused on ministry outputs first, and then business concepts were considered to make these ministry outputs sustainable. The next two chapters begin with a different focus, that of helping poor people to increase incomes or obtain employment. The concepts of business incubators and micro credit are introduced, with various means of promoting micro credit described in some detail.

The focus of this book is somewhat different from the thousands of articles related to micro finance on the Internet and elsewhere, because we begin with a focus on the target group. If we consider the very poor people, the first thing we notice is that not all of them want a loan, nor can they handle a loan. So we do not impose on them a credit model, but consider the possibility of an equity model as well, the promotion of business where they are an employee, but not involved in management. This we call the business incubator paradigm, which can be considered "micro finance," but not "micro credit," because the financed part is equity rather than leverage.

Another way the focus of this book is very different from other presentations is that it is not promoting a model for growing programs. The popular concept called "scaling up" has actually brought very negative consequences for many organizations, as organizational objectives are sacrificed on the altar of growth. Organizations started to help the poor change their focus to more wealthy populations, and organizations started to help the church slowly become completely secular social service agencies, just to get bigger. Bigger is not necessarily better, and it is possible to organize completely sustainable micro finance projects on a very small scale, and with limited capital.

Many development organizations that work in the area of micro finance were started within the church, and with an ethos of simplicity and modest lifestyle. This changed with the boom in micro finance in the 1990s. The salaries of managers of organizations that promote themselves based on help for the poor, listed for all to see at www.guidestar.com, have graduated to the world of big business. For example, in one Christian micro credit agency, the salary of their regional director went from $15,000 to $150,000 in a period of less than ten years. The high cost structure of many of these organizations means that government and international agency money is necessary for survival, just to pay U.S. salaries. External funding from governments and other international institutions moves them further and further away from a focus on either the poor or the church.

Given this sad history, we begin with a commitment to purpose, having seen how easy it is for a desire to help others to be converted into a focus on helping ourselves. We begin with a belief that economic projects can be started and managed with church involvement, and stay integrated with church outreach. We begin with a concern about accepting the agenda that is popular with governments and international funding institutions. We also begin with an emphasis of focus on the target group, and defining program based on needs rather than on an external agenda promoted by others.

The temptation to start with an external agenda is natural, as models that have been developed in other contexts can be implemented by copying what was done elsewhere. The problem with this franchise approach to economic development is that it only works when the clients can be adjusted to fit the program, rather than the program adjusted to fit the clients. For example, many good models exist to help people who sell goods in the market, but these only work well for people who have businesses in the market. This is one of the reasons why so much "micro enterprise promotion" is currently concentrated in markets–that is where many organizations want to find their clients. The fact that clients are selected based on their fit with the definitions of the programs is also why so few micro finance programs are integrated with the church. Church members often do not qualify because they do not live in the right area, or do not have prior business experience. The predetermined service methodology has excluded them.

How different when the program definition begins with definition of the needs of the people being served! If the purpose of the program is to serve the people, it is only logical to start with an evaluation of what the people need, and then apply the best methodology for their situation, to increase income and create permanent employment through productive economic activity.

The possibility of using revolving loan or micro credit methodology is a popular alternative because it can generate, through charging fees and/or interest, the basis for the long-term sustainability of the program. It is dependent, however, on the assumption that people or groups of people have viable existing enterprises or business proposals that can be successful through loan financing. When the people we are trying to serve do not have an existing enterprise, or even a proposal for a viable business, other micro finance methods must be created to help them. A combination of financing methodologies, accompanied by non-financial services targeted at helping with daily business management, controlling costs, obtaining adequate prices, etc. has proven to be the best way to help with business and program success.

The goal, at the community level, is to generate increased income and permanent employment for the poor through productive activity that is viable in the real world marketplace. It is important also to consider a secondary goal of making the program itself sustainable, so that funds can be recycled and service delivery continue without continual dependence on donations. From the start, the resources that the church has, including the volunteer assistance of professionals, can be combined with outside resources to promote a focus on transformation, not just of the economic situation, but also of the social and spiritual environment. What makes church-based micro finance different from other organizations is that it is focused on the needs of a target group that usually includes the very poor, and it is also integrated with the evangelistic and discipleship ministry of the church.

The focus on the poor usually means that this group is not eligible for assistance from other programs. This is because the very poor do not have the financial collateral or job/business experience that is required for entry into most government or international agency micro credit programs. Church-based programs are generally dealing with a more risky population, but also have some distinct advantages. First, the church has deep roots in the community in which it works, and knows the people and their history. Second, the volunteer participation of church members in training, visitation, consulting, and helping with small projects is a significant resource for dealing with projects that require a lot of assistance. Thirdly, the methodologies that can be applied, with a process of graduating from very small projects to larger and larger ventures, based on success over time, helps to minimize risk and identify entrepreneurs who are able to increase the size and profitability of their businesses.

Analysis of the target group

The first common discovery that is made in studying the needs of the people to be served is that, in many cases, the potential clients are not ready for the discipline required for a loan program. Again, this is often because church programs are targeted at very poor populations that may have difficulty in conceptualizing a profitable business. They would not know what to do with a loan.

The analysis should consider the people's needs, environment, and also the resources that they have. Evaluation of the needs includes identification of problems with health, safety and security, logistics, and educational background. Sometimes it may be necessary to address problems discovered in these areas before embarking on micro finance activities. For example, if crime is rampant in a specific community, the consideration of how to protect machinery or tools for a business has to be discussed as a first priority. If potential clients cannot read and write, specialized training may be needed prior to implementing a business, to prepare them for the need to account for and control money.

The environment of the target group includes issues such as access to raw materials for production, transportation access, marketing channels, local competition, and other factors that play a role in the success of a productive economic activity in that area. The resources of the group include their job experience, their assets, their formal and informal education, their history of access to credit, and their entrepreneurial orientation.

It is often the case that people have had some experience in subsidized economic activities, such as handicrafts, sewing projects for women or communal projects with some connection to business. This background could be helpful if the projects were viable, but could also be a negative factor if the activity were subsidized. Often expectations are created through these types of projects that economic development is just another form of hidden handout, and that there is no need to be concerned about critical issues such as quality, oversight and productivity. It is very important to communicate to potential clients that the micro finance approach being proposed is dependent on viable enterprises and hard work.

Selecting a Finance Methodology

The methodology should be chosen to respond to the needs of a specific target group, and these needs may change over time. That is why the presentation of micro finance models in this book is eclectic, a toolbox that can be combined to stimulate a process of graduation through successive levels of growth in the life of a business, meeting the changing demands of the clients. There are cases where poor people, with no previous experience in business and without collateral, have begun with training in a business incubator, bought the assets with a small community bank loan, expanded and added employees with a solidarity loan, bought new equipment with an individual loan, and then gone into the formal banking system to obtain commercial loans. This is the exception rather than the rule, but it can happen. The following section presents financing methodologies applicable at these succeeding levels.

Level 1
Business Incubators

This is a model that has evolved internally in many church contexts in response to the desperate need to create employment for people in the church community. A business is proposed, usually one in which church members have had experience, and seed capital is obtained to fund this business. The church or a church-related committee is the owner and operator of the business, and the people who are working in it are treated as employees. As the business proves its viability, the profits are used to pay back the initial capital that was invested. If the people who are employed in the business demonstrate the capacity to run it, they are often encouraged to buy the business, and the funds invested in the business (equity) are converted into a loan (leverage), so that the initial investors get their funds back, or the pool that exists to help in business start-ups can be used to help other people. For example, a church with a lot of women who are unemployed or underemployed sets up a small bakery, and once it is working, the five women who operate it decide to "buy out" the business by a commitment to pay back the invested capital. Or a church with a group of unemployed men who know how to do upholstery funds a business to help them get started, and as they begin to generate a profit, they decided to buy the business.

This methodology is often applied in Christian outreach with special populations that need employment, such as street adolescents, people recovering from substance abuse, and ex prisoners, all of whom have great difficulty in obtaining employment. If a niche business can be identified that can be operated on an individual basis, this approach creates an alternative for setting people up with a job, even if they know very little about business. Successful examples include teaching street girls how to make stuffed animals for export markets, teaching recuperated drug addicts how to make tortilla presses for local markets in Mexico, teaching women ex-convicts how to make artisan products, and teaching male ex-convicts how to organize and run specialized cottage industries of various types.

The important issue with all of these cases is to identify a business plan that provides for a viable enterprise, and that can be taught. The design of the business must provide for opportunities that can be supervised initially from the outside, by people not involved full time in the business. The design must also provide the opportunity to be able to discontinue the participation of certain people, or withdraw the assets from the business, in the case that the proposed clients cannot demonstrate interest or ability in making it work. This is why they are initially employees, not owners of the business. That the business in not theirs to do with as they please is a most important issue to clarify; it is their hard work and entrepreneurial input that will be key in making the business successful.

The key requirements for a business incubator project include the definition of the productive economic activity, prices, costs, and a definition of who is responsible for daily operation. A great deal of training is also often part of this model, as the participants do not necessarily have a background to understand production requirements, technology, and markets. In many cases, the training phase is funded by a ministry project addressing the needs of specific targeted populations, and the incubator project can be built on a foundation of services provided by another group working with prisons, street children, drug addicts, etc.

A variety of businesses have been created through this methodology, and the entrepreneurship of the person or group that initiates projects is another key factor. For example, funding projects related to rural agriculture in developing countries is avoided by most international micro finance institutions, as it is considered too risky for business investment even though that is where many of the poor happen to live. An entire range of incubator business approaches exists for rural agriculture, that have been developed through specialized training, emphasis on special technologies, alternative production inputs, and specialized niche marketing. Some involve group enterprises for organic crop production, oriented to export markets. In many cases the simple organization of a rural transport service has proven to be profitable, as well as benefiting producers, consumers, and passengers. Group business to lower costs by bulk purchasing, or raise prices by cooperative marketing schemes, have also been successfully funded through business incubator approaches.

Sometimes the business incubator projects require more capital than small loan programs, especially when the business funded is targeted at a group of people. However, the benefits may also be greater when the entire group is taken into account, and the security of the funding is based on the fact that individuals do not hold ownership of the project. Critical management decisions can be made, and changes to the business approach can be implemented in the process of the evolution of the business.

Level 2
Community Banking

Community or village banking is the name given to a decentralized lending model where very poor people, without business experience or collateral, can be provided small amounts of capital based on control and supervision by their peers. This method provides a mechanism to provide funding with minimal risk that will permit poor people to start or expand cottage enterprises, and grow them through successive loans of increasing amounts. The requirement for paying back the loan is accompanied by a defined deposit to a savings account. The provision of small amounts of capital also helps to identify the entrepreneurs in the group, who with greater assistance might be able to create wealth and employment for others in the community. This approach is well suited for evangelism and discipleship activity, and has been applied with success to many diverse contexts.

There are eight principles that are important in organizing community banks of between 15 and 50 participants:

1. There must be an organized group of some kind, comprised of people who are socially connected in some way. Again, the church provides an excellent context for group organization.
2. There must be an autonomous process of selection for the participants of the group, as it is critical that people in the group be considered by each other to be responsible, because all assume the risk of default for each other's loans. The selection process in itself may be the most important issue in the success of the projects, as people will not want to be with others who have a track record of irresponsibility.
3. Everyone in the group must accept that the activities to be funded will be productive economic businesses that generate income, and not personal consumption. Generally, the type of activity funded by the small loans provided by community banks is household projects that increase incomes, especially for women. In some cases, members of community banks pool their loans and work on projects together.
4. Any activity funded in the group has to be evaluated by the group and receive prior approval before funding.
5. Loans will be provided in cycles with amounts increas-

ing, but the ability to continue receiving larger loans is conditional on paying the previous amount.

6. A small deposit to a locally controlled savings account will be requested in addition to each loan payment. Savings will be considered as loan collateral, but also be available for emergencies, and to replace the need for a loan when a person exits from the program.

   Though savings is often proposed as a source of funds for micro finance, the community bank is one of the only contexts where organized savings pools can be encouraged on a formal basis, and then only when managed by the clients themselves. Full-scale programs of managing savings are difficult to manage, and in most places only the government authorities can authorize a program for holding deposits from the public. The hurdle rate for doing this is often in excess of millions of dollars, and also requires holding a deposit with the Central Bank, presenting detailed reports, and conforming to other government rules and regulations. This has proven to be very difficult for development organizations, and has also resulted in some giving up their focus on the poor to become commercial banks.

7. The interest rate will be equal to or more than market rates, subject to the decision of the group.

8. Governance of the community bank is democratic, and is clearly spelled out in the rules and regulations that all have been provided. This methodology requires a good deal of community organization prior to the financing of projects, but once the group is operating, it involves only periodic supervision from the outside. In many cases the full-time staff supervising the programs only show up for monthly group meetings, and may visit some projects, but not necessarily all of them. The assumption is that the members of the group will take on assistance and supervisory roles for each other.

From the perspective of the entity that is organizing programs, the community bank is viewed as only one loan. All of the members are obligated to pay for it. What happens in reality is that as savings payments accumulate with loan payments, the savings amount of the members replaces the externally injected loan funds in one or two years, so that the lending activity at the community bank level can continue even as the initial amount is completely paid back.

The objectives of the community banks are both financial and social, as are the definitions of the indicators used to measure impact. One important indicator is the level of cooperation of people involved in small business activity, and often the phenomenon of these people helping each other has more impact than the loan itself. Other financial indicators, like payment record for both capital and interest, the amounts of savings that have been deposited, and the level of arrears are often very important. The average loan size for a community bank loan in Latin America is around $50, so this is a program that can operate in very poor environments.

The community bank model is considered to be an efficient form of providing capital to poor people at a low administrative cost per person. The model is of benefit to poor people in allowing them the capacity to start and grow small business activities, and successively become eligible for greater amounts of capital based on a track record that they create for themselves.

Level 3
Solidarity Groups

Another model for organizing revolving loan programs is the solidarity group,. the loan clients with little or no business experience or loan collateral. In this approach, organize themselves in groups of 5 to 10 people, based on a common business activity or geographic proximity. As members of the group, they all sign a loan contract for each other, taking responsibility for the whole group payment as well as for their own. As in the case of community banking, this will naturally require investigation by group members prior to the formation of a group, and the elimination of prospects unlikely to pay.

The requirement of solidarity with others in the selection process in effect guarantees the loan, as poor candidates will be eliminated by their peers. Also in the case of collecting payments, this peer pressure to pay on time is helpful in obtaining a good payment record. A problem with late payments of any member group is a problem for the rest of the group, because they will be required to pay.

Solidarity groups also focus on helping each other in production, marketing, and organization. The small groups meet periodically to share how their businesses are going, and this facilitates supervision from the outside entity, as the project promoter can attend these meetings, and follow them up with visits to businesses that might be experiencing difficulties.

As with community banking, there are many manuals and guides available for defining specific procedures for organizing, funding, supervising, and collecting funds from solidarity groups. It is important to define how a group governs itself, who calls meetings, how collections are made, and how both personal and group documentation is written. The requirements for supervision must also be planned in advance, with specific impact indicators that not only evaluate the financial areas, but how solidarity requirements might have generated cooperation and sharing. The average size loan with solidarity groups in Latin America is around $200, and there are also many solidarity schemes that provide growing amounts of capital for subsequent loans.

Level 4
Individual Loans

The community bank and solidarity loan programs described above are revolving loan methodologies. The basic instrument or development tool used for these, and the individual loan program, is a loan. Revolving loan methodologies have in common the following principles:

- The loan must be paid back; it is not a hidden handout.
- Therefore, the funded project must generate a profit.
- This is facilitated by a program of evaluation and supervision.
- The cost of the program has to be covered by client fees or interest.
- Capital that is paid back is recycled to other people.

The implementation of these principles leads to two cycles of sustainability. At the level of individuals and families, the business activity provides them with sustainable resources. As they pay the "rental fee" for the asset they are using, or the interest, this guarantees the financial sustainability of the entity that is providing the loans, paying for staff and services. In the case of community banks and solidarity groups, the loan to the group is seen as one loan, even though it is portioned out to many people, and the fee related to the loan pays for the one project supervisor assigned to the group, plus covers other costs.

The provision of capital to an individual person is perhaps the methodology most expected, but least evident, in programs that focus on the needs of the poor. This is generally a level where some type of guarantee would be required to obtain a loan, and not many people may qualify. It is also a level where bigger loans would be required, and organizations that have the funds to help the poor will generally desire to give many small loans to many people rather than few larger loans to a few people.

Individual loans require not only guarantees, but also a business plan that demonstrates how funds will be used. The most important factor in evaluating a business plan is looking at the market projections, because it is far easier to make things than to sell them, especially at a good price. In general, a successful individual loan will exhibit some competitive advantage that makes it stand out from other similar businesses.

The truth about success in small business is that it depends to a large extent on the entrepreneurial nature of the person operating the business. Unfortunately, the definition of "entrepreneurship" is hard to evaluate. That is why the graduation from prior levels of community banking or solidarity group lending is such a great foundation for funding individual loans. For example, a rural tailor in Honduras grew his business from one sewing machine to hundreds by focusing on making a special type of blue jeans.

People who can do this often make money for themselves in the process, but they also create a great many benefits for others through increasing production and employment for other poor people. Social benefits are expanded, along with permanent jobs. This does not mean that those whose businesses stay small have failed. Many clients of solidarity groups do not desire to expand their business beyond cottage industries, and are happy not to have more employees and more problems that come from more business. Many clients of community banks want only to increase household income through their small loans, and have no plans for anything beyond that. They appreciate having a savings account available, but plan to leave it alone for emergencies, not access it for further expansion.

Chapter 8

Administrative Organization of Micro-Enterprise Programs

T The management of financial programs to promote economic development requires professional administrative organization. This chapter addresses many of the foundational issues, and these will need to be applied within the context of the particular environment where the project is being implemented.

Limiting the program to specific commercial activity

The economic development programs are created to help the poor to increase income and create permanent employment through investment in productive economic activity. By definition, this would exclude not only illegal and unethical activity, but also the financing of consumption, celebration, personal emergencies, and any other expenditure not related to productive activity. A definition about the expectations for projects is needed not only to protect the organization that is providing the financing and promote recovery of the funds based on proper investment, but also to prevent that the client become trapped in debt, and help him/her to fend off requests for money from family and friends.

The requirement to invest only in productive activity that is viable in the real world marketplace may exclude certain potential beneficiaries, and it should be noted that micro finance methodologies might exclude certain needy populations. It is not possible to impact through these programs the "poorest of the poor" that are unable to be economically active due to health problems, substance abuse, or even who do not want to work. Some academics and fund raisers who promote micro finance without regard to the limitations of the methodology seem to believe that it is a solution for everyone, and go so far as to propose that programs should not worry about how financing will be used, "because the poor can evaluate how to invest better than outsiders can." The statement sounds good, but is actually ridiculous, unfortunately the basis for many failed programs. It trivializes the difficulty of creating a successful business, and at the same time ignores the reality that we all face that there are always things we want to buy, even if we don't really need them. The saying in Spanish is: "Lo que no nos cuesta, hacemos fiesta." If it didn't cost me anything, let's have a party. Again, since the purpose of the program is to promote sustainability, we need to be concerned that viable projects be funded. Economic development is the goal, not just investing in projects, and unsuccessful projects can result in the supposed beneficiaries being worse off after "financial assistance." Conditions must be established to facilitate a process of transformation of a financial asset into a business project that is profitable in a competitive environment.

Source of capital

Generally the economic development programs begin with donated capital that comes for various sources. Special financing from specific donors often provides the seed funding, and may be matched by local donations. Sometimes funds are also available from local organizations and even the government, as there is considerable interest in the area of micro finance.

The organizations providing the capital may have an interest in a specific target group, or a defined geographical area, or in some other characteristic of the target population. Such definitions must be carefully considered in establishing policies for the program. Once the program has a track record of successful operation, it may be possible to access additional funds from other such donors. This also needs to be taken into account when the program is designed, so an awareness of project criteria and reporting requirements of future possible donors can be taken into account, laying the groundwork for growth through proposals for additional funding.

Present and potential donors may also affect financing policies to some extent. The establishment of financing policy always requires a balancing act: the desire to help the poor and the desire to promote financial sustainability of operations. The requirement to operate the program without a deficit impacts not only how much risk can be taken with client projects, but also other issues such as geographical focus and ability to require participation in technical training prior to approval of projects.

If the objective of the program is to help the poor and promote Christian witness, there is also the possibility that conditions defined by potential funding sources may be unacceptable. It is better for the program to stay small and maintain its objectives than to grow into something different than it was created to be.

Defining Requirements for Projects

The programs are designed to adapt to the needs of the potential clients in the target group. In many cases, training is required, and a graduation process may be anticipated from business incubators to community banks, to solidarity groups, and on to individual projects, at every level with more rigorous requirements and with higher levels of complexity.

The programs that begin with a group focus, as opposed to an individual focus, generally require:

- That the people comprising the group have demonstrated experience of working together with others, perhaps on other types of projects.
- That there be a commitment of solidarity in relation to the financial obligations, to take responsibility of the payment for the whole group.
- That the members be from a similar social and economic population.
- That the members have demonstrated responsibility, honoring of commitments, moral character, and interest in their personal development.
- That there be sufficient definition of leadership in the group to manage funds and oversee productive econom-

ic activity.
- That there be positive references about the group in its community and from the church.
- That members of the group have some technical experience or training in the economic activity to be funded.
- That all persons with the responsibility for paying back the funds be involved in the economic activity as their principal source of income.
- That all persons with the responsibility of paying back the funds be free from personal debts and financial commitments to other financial organizations.

It is also important that potential clients commit to participate in technical training programs, and the attendance and participation in such programs is often a requirement for project approval. Technical training will be described in more detail in the next chapter.

Before obtaining financial assistance, potential clients must also commit to the following principles:

- To use the resources provided for productive activity in cottage industry, services, commerce, or agriculture and not to use them for personal consumption, family emergencies, special events, or any illegal activity.
- To use funds for the project defined in the application process. If the person decides to use funds for activities other than those specified in the application, it will be grounds for immediate return of the capital. It is not acceptable to change approved business plans and still receive funding.
- To become eligible for additional capital, the existing capital or loans must first be paid back. Timely compliance with payment commitments will be a critical factor in analyzing any new proposal.
- For those involved in a disciplined savings program, the

commitment that they will also reinvest their savings in their business activity.

- Willingness to participate in training programs and opportunities to cooperate and share with other business clients.
- The evidence of basic financial systems in their businesses that allows them to evaluate how the business is doing financially, and also shows evidence of responsible controls. Systems may be very simple, but should exist in some form.
- The demonstration of an attitude of cooperation with program field personnel when they visit their business, allowing the access to the projects and all documentation related to its operation.

The Recruiting Process

The contact with the potential person or group usually begins through the church, and in an outreach project that the church is promoting. Many programs have a regular introductory talk for prospective clients that includes a general description of how to get involved, what type of projects are funded, requirements, and definition of the specific steps involved to apply for entry into the program.

A one-page information form is useful at this level, that allows project management to evaluate quickly whether the individuals or groups that want to get involved would qualify, or have a realistic business idea. It is at this level that those desiring to receive assistance can form groups, but who can only do so as part of a group. Program staff and volunteers from the church are often involved at this stage, not only in organizing potential business incubator, community bank, or solidarity groups, but also helping with the definition of the business idea, and providing a sounding board on what kinds of projects might be viable.

Often people who present the initial information form are hunting for money, with little business background or even interest in implementing a project. If they cannot even describe the type of project they would like to promote, and how it functions, they probably should not be allowed loan funding. Perhaps they can be included in technical training, or begin by helping in an incubator project. The approval process must filter all requests for assistance and help the organization to focus time only on analyzing potential projects that have success possibilities.

Projects that demonstrate possibilities should be allowed further consideration through a defined application form. This form should include data about the project, location, background, and principals. The amount to be invested and payment plan should be accompanied by a business plan that, at a minimum, specifies market assumptions related to price and quantity, and includes a definition of the cost of the goods sold. A major misconception, in the informal sector, is to confuse cash flow with profit, and the application form should be created to sort this out, and identify the margin that is important, not only for the well-being of the client, but for pay back of the capital.

The evaluation of the information not only allows for analysis of viability, but is also a test of the capacity of the client to know the business. Information about the cost of input can easily be evaluated. Sales projections are more difficult to assess, but pricing information can be corroborated. The most important issue generally is the marketing, and assumptions related to quantity sold and retail margins are often highly overstated. A simple analysis is all that is needed to identify this problem.

Except for the case of the community banks, this duty of evaluating applications falls to the project supervisor, frequently with assistance of volunteers in the church. He/she must decide which applications look promising, and pass them on to the credit committee. In the case of community banks, a committee of bank members themselves does the evaluation of applications.

General Program Policies

The overall policies for the program are defined by the board, and need to be evaluated periodically as the program matures. The church leadership also plays a role in defining these policies, and sometimes donors providing the initial capital are also involved. As the board assumes the responsibility for the supervision of the organization, it is responsible for the continual evaluation of program policy.

The amounts of capital or loans provided vary according to methodology, and also depend on the level of development in a given country. There are places where a loan of $50 can be sufficient to start a business, and other places where an investment of ten times that much is not enough to start anything. It is impossible to define the amount of funds needed to start a business without taking into account the context. A rule of thumb in developing countries is that community bank loans start at around $50 per client, solidarity loans at $200 per client, and individual loans at $1,000 per client. Investment in incubators depends also on whether they are for individuals or groups. It should be noted that the limitations on the size of a loan or invested capital impacts the costs and capacity of the organization to place funds. For example, a policy prescribing very small loans will mean that project supervisors need to be assigned many projects to visit, whereas larger projects will require fewer projects per supervisor, to be able to promote sustainability based on a return on capital.

A related policy issue is whether the same client can obtain multiple loans. On the one hand, helping one business grow, even from an incubator stage, is consistent with the idea of graduation between methodologies, and increases in amounts funded are accompanied by some decrease in risk, and the project is well known. On the other hand, the same amount of funding could be used to help others. Perhaps the answer to this question resides in an analysis of the social impact resulting from increased capital. Within each methodology, and between methodologies, there is flexibility to provide more capital for a project. But the basis for doing so should be to evaluate first what the impact is of subsequent funding in terms of increased income, more jobs, and more production. If this is not done, a dependence on outside funding may be created by subsequent financing, and the business may actually become increasingly less viable through outside assistance, needing a loan to survive.

Policies related to repayment plans also vary according to methodology, and also according to the type of activity being funded. The payment plan is usually defined in relation to the cash flow generated through the funded project. In most cases, a monthly payment cycle is possible, and makes a habit of paying the funding on time. In fact, when initial grace periods are allowed, this can have the detrimental effect of the client forgetting about the vital need to make a payment. Agricultural projects present a special case, where income is generated at harvest time, but must also be stored in some cases to guarantee better prices. Even with agriculture, it is better to create a pattern of payments, perhaps with a balloon payback when the harvest is sold, to promote the habit of setting aside some money to pay back capital. It is also a good idea to program payments based on a substantial amount of the profit margin anticipated, not only to permit a better payment record through a shorter pay off period, but also to be allowed to recycle capital to other worthy projects to help other people.

Policies for payment on business incubators often involve conversion of invested equity into a stream of loan payments. A portion of net revenues is required at the initial phase, as a rental fee on the monies provided and a payment to cover the costs of supervision and oversight. As employees take over administration, they can buy out the business by converting the invested equity into a loan.

Interest rate policy is another area where the equilibrium must be found between the good of the client and the sustainability of the organization. The amount charged must be sufficient to cover costs of placement, supervision and collection: the total service delivery costs of the entity providing the capital. It must also provide a reserve for bad debts, and enough to offset inflation and thereby conserve the real value of the fund. At the same time, the costs must be bearable by the client, at a reasonable rate compared to local financial markets. A point of reference in defining what is "reasonable" is the market rate of interest. An interest rate similar to the formal banking system helps also to eliminate requests for funding for people who actually have access to such funding, and only would be looking for lower cost funds. Loan prospects in the high-risk informal sector have no access to such rates. They often compare them to the "loan shark" rates available in their environment, and find the interest of rates offered by economic development organizations to be very low.

It is periodically necessary to evaluate interest rate calculations, taking into account both a revised calculation of the costs of services, a revised analysis of uncollectable accounts, and an estimation of inflation or devaluation. Such a review should be made at least on an annual basis, and recommendations for adjustments presented at board level. For community banks, an additional amount is sometimes charged, with group concurrence, to provide an emergency fund for members.

The policies for collection often include some type of collateral for recuperation of capital, falling into one of four categories:

- *Mortgage guarantee* – land, buildings and houses with legal documentation that can be registered.
- *Equipment collateral* – tangible assets that are described in loan documentation, and are transferred if payment commitments are not made.
- *Leasing contracts* – when bought by loan proceeds or with organization funds, the equipment is held in the name of the organization until payment is made.
- *Cosigners* – other people with defined income who sign as responsible parties to the loan, and who have to pay it back if the principal does not.

The actual practice of collection through loan collateral is very difficult, and the collateral is most useful in creating a serious image of the project, and the need to pay back capital. The specific requirements for collateral depend on the local context. In some countries it is illegal to use production equipment as collateral, for example, because it would take away the person's form of earning a livelihood. So it would not be possible to take a sewing machine, but one could instead assign a television set as the guarantee.

The client is always provided a payment plan, and also a tentative plan for monitoring and supervision of the project. In some cases the project supervisor goes with the client at the moment of fund disbursement to buy equipment and raw materials, and to help to assure that the investment plan is being followed. Whatever the means used to disburse funds, it is recognized that decisions made in the first few weeks after disbursement are very critical. The investment in the project is important, but the success of that investment depends, to a great extent, on prior investment in training, orientation, and preparation of the client.

Chapter 9

Training to Promote
the Sustainability
of Client Economic Activity

The presentation of micro finance methodologies often focuses on the technical requirements of the service delivery program. The sustainability of the program is important, but not as important as the sustainability of the underlying economic activity that is funded. For example, if a specific program has all of the systems and controls to promote that loans are collected on time but clients, to pay the loans, have to sell their assets or obtain funding from higher costs loan sharks, this is not success. And if clients cannot demonstrate a sustainable business operation after receiving capital, but rather must continue to obtain injections of funds to keep their business going, the benefits of the program are minimal. The financial success of economic development programs to help the poor should be measured principally in terms of self-reliant client projects.

The most important issue in facilitating successful client projects is the skill of small business managers.

Frequently the assumption of the small business opera-tors in the informal sector is that they can succeed with low standards that result in a poor quality product with very small margins, sold in a market already flooded with such products. Again, the most common examples of this in church projects are the sewing "businesses" organized for women, where all inputs of production are subsi-dized, products are made that cannot compete in the real world marketplace due to poor quality, and where there is little discipline in relating costs to prices. The problem is not just that these businesses fail, but that many people experience another personal failure, as expectations of employment or income are shattered. Training in basic business concepts is very important to prepare people adequately for economic activity that can generate gen-uine profits.

Requirements of the Clients
Before Financing is Provided

The application form is a test of whether a potential client has the capacity to organize and administer a small busi-ness. The applicant must be able to describe in detail the basic ingredients of the economic activity, costs, produc-tion process, and market prices. If they are not able to do so, they will need help.

Others can help them to fill in the form: family mem-bers, neighbors, people in the community or the church. If program staff helps to fill in the necessary information, they should do so with a conscious effort to use this oppor-tunity to identify the areas where the potential client or client group needs technical training, and make pre-project training a requirement for approval of the project.

The topic of pre-project training is a much-debated issue in organizations that promote economic development. One point of view is that small business entrepreneurs do not need training, because they know much better than outsiders how to use their money, so financing should be provided without asking many questions. This view is popular not only for its egalitarian focus, but also because it implies that organizations do not have to invest in training programs, and thus can be easier to sustain financially, without having that burden.

On the other extreme is the view that training inputs, both formal and informal, are actually as important, or more important than the financing itself, which basically provides the incentive for people to accept constructive recommendations in how their business is managed. For example, to teach an entrepreneur the difference between profit and cash flow helps them with their entire business, not just with payback of a loan. From this perspective, the need for training programs is seen as the most valuable tool for helping the poor be successful in the complex world of business. This may be difficult to prove through empirical studies, as the attitude of potential clients toward required classes is often similar to children's attitude towards school. But they learn much that is important, even if they do not recognize it themselves.

Every new program for helping the poor through economic programs needs to consider both perspectives. The evaluation and valuation of what people already know is important, and given the costs related to training, it may be necessary to limit the investment in educational programs, and target it at critical areas of need. But these critical areas cannot be ignored, and therefore some basic training programs should generally be incorporated in the program, and considered as part of the costs that must be covered by program revenue. Furthermore, if subsidies can be obtained from other sources for training, or partnerships crafted with other organizations that provide educational programs, these should also be sought out. It should also be noted that the formal training programs provide good opportunities to integrate Christian witness into the program.

There are three areas of training that have proven to be critical to the success of small business programs, and that can also be easily organized into three training modules:

1- General administration of the business for entrepreneurs, with an introduction of the program of the organization and how it operates.
2- Principles of marketing and sales.
3- Cost control and basic accounting or record keeping.

These modules can be organized in three separate sessions, and provided at a time that does not take potential clients away from their business. For example, evening or Saturday afternoon sessions of 2 to 3 hours can be scheduled at a place that is easily accessible, often the church itself. In some contexts it may be necessary to encourage people to bring children in the cases where they will be assisting with reading or mathematics; many potential clients may not be able to read or write. Formal training sessions are often taught by program staff or church volunteers, and it is extremely important that trainers be well prepared. Written materials and handouts are important not only for helping in presentations, but also to standardize the content of the courses, and promote a minimal quality of presentation. It is very important to end every training module with an evaluation by the students, to make sure that the training is meeting its objectives. A very common problem identified in evaluations is that the trainers, with their university education, have not been able to simplify concepts enough for potential clients with little education. Efforts must continually be made to assure that teaching is understandable. A balance must also be sought to promote a high quality education with low available resources.

The introductory module is on general administrative principles, and can also be used to present in detail all of the requirements for obtaining funding, and specific expectations for potential clients. After the objectives of the program have been discussed, the Biblical basis of promoting productive economic activity can be presented, with Jesus as an example of a small business entrepreneur who understands the environment of business. Commercial organization can be presented from a human and ethical perspective, with the goals of providing for family, for living in a responsible and honorable fashion, and for also working hard to assure that the business is successful. The first session can be offered for those who are considering involvement in the program.

Recommended Topics of Workshop #1
General Administration for Entrepreneurs

1- Why are we here? Start with Biblical reflections on the purpose of the program in relation to God's plan for our lives, with a focus on the concept of work, that God worked, and wants us to be able to work to provide our daily bread.

2- Economic development as a strategy to help people: expectations of social and community outputs such as increased income, employment creation, production, and other benefits.

3- Expectations at the project level: successful businesses, competent administration, ethical practices, and payment of capital and related fees.

4- Explanation of the specific requirements for individuals or groups, including a detailed presentation of the application process and next steps.

5- What is an entrepreneur? How the success of the business depends on the innovation and commitment of the applicant.

6- What are critical administrative areas in a business? The importance of understanding markets, and implementing basic controls, concluding with promotion of attendance at the next two modules.

The second module is about marketing. What does the potential client need to know about the market? The most common problem is that few people seem to distinguish between production and sales in their analysis of their business activity. It is easy to determine how many shoes, shirts, or bags of beans can be produced with outside funding, but distribution systems for all of these are more complex, and prices differ considerably in relation to where and when these products are sold. It is often the case that the distribution decisions are critical in the success of enterprises in the informal sector.

Recommended Topics of Workshop #2
Understanding Sales and Markets

1- Biblical reflection on the business that Paul used to support his ministry, how he encouraged people to work, that his own work was as a leather craftsman, that he was able to support himself by making and selling leather tents, and that he believed in doing good work, as to the Lord.

2- The importance of markets, and the need to understand better our own markets for products or services. Introduce the four critical elements of marketing: product, price, place (distribution), and promotion.

3- Identify the conditions that we require for adequate sales levels. What are our starting assumptions?

4- How can we change the marketing mix to increase sales, improve margins, stabilize sales over time, take advantage of seasonal or special opportunities, and cooperate with others?

5- The presentation of ideas and potential strategies to help, depending on the context. The instructor will need to get information on the project proposals presented by the pupils to prepare this segment.

6- The complications generated when businesses provide credit to sell their products, and an analysis of how to avoid doing so, or how to do this and make sure you get paid.

7- Promotion of innovation in marketing: using the contacts with new friends from the workshop itself to sell products, alternatives for export, product modification, sources of information, etc.

Through the training in basic marketing, the potential clients should be encouraged to think about their costs and prices, and consider alternatives for distribution of their product that would allow them an increased percentage of the total retail margin. They should also consider changes in their product that would make it more marketable, and ways to cooperate with others who could help them in improving quality. The analysis of markets is a significant part of their application process, and this training should also help them to finish the written form that is required for obtaining assistance.

Aside from marketing, the other biggest problem of the small businessperson is lack of adequate financial controls. As was mentioned before, a chronic problem is the confusion between cash flow and profits, the perception that because money is coming into the business, money is being made. But often the amount coming into the business is less than the cost of what is being sold, and this is especially true with the injection of outside capital. So the purpose of the training module on control and basic accounting is to help potential clients develop systems that they can manage to evaluate the performance of their business, to ascertain if products they make are profitable or not, and to allow them to measure how they are doing on a daily basis.

This requires a system for recording revenues and expenditures. At the beginning of a project, some of the expenditures are related to investment in equipment, but some also may be part of the "cost of goods sold" of products. This concept must be introduced to allow clients to determine profit margins. The module should be presented with cases and examples, and the proposition of simple systems for analysis. It also needs to be developed with a sensibility of the types of business activity represented in the group, as control systems depend to a great extent on the type of business being considered.

Specific recommendations need to be as simplified as possible. For example, for people who do not read or write, a system of pockets can be proposed, with one daily transfer from revenue pocket to the expense pocket, and amounts noted at that time, perhaps with the help of a child or a friend that has had some schooling.

Recommended Topics for Workshop #3
Cash Control and Basic Accounting

1- Biblical reflection on the statements that Jesus makes about managing a loan (parable of the talents) and about building a tower. The need for careful analysis and planning for a successful project.
2- Administrative control – the definition of mechanisms for planning and control. What are we really interested in measuring?
3- The design of basic registry systems that can define revenue and expense on a daily basis. The instructor will have to plan this in relation to the participants. It is especially important not to impose on them double entry bookkeeping or other complex systems that an instructor may have learned at the university.
4- Cost analysis to determine where net margins are being generated, on the basis of a product, product mix, service, etc. In some cases, a simple break-even analysis may be used.
5- Definition of key concepts: working capital, cost of goods sold, and owner equity. It is also important to define the salary expectations of the entrepreneur as part of the costs of operations, as this is often left out of the equation when determining profitability.
6- The need to put aside the amounts necessary to pay back capital and the fee for using the capital, i.e. interest.
7- The additional goal of reinvesting a certain amount in the business so that it can grow.

For training programs to be successful, there also must be a training program for the trainers. The best teachers will be those who know the context where the pupils come from, and who also have the time to visit them personally. It is important to note, in the contexts of developing countries, that people with recognized degrees are often the least qualified to do client training, as they may have learned everything through a rote learning method that is very difficult to apply in the informal sector. For example, a session that begins with the definition of "credit and debit" copied on the blackboard is probably worthless.

It is also important that trainers communicate an enthusiasm for the topic. Training programs are sometimes begun with a shared vision, but then the pace of operational activity kicks in. The need to focus on projects in arrears, or place more funds, or increase the load of clients to be supervised squeezes out all time for training. The participant evaluations will identify when the trainer has lost interest, or when the training program has become an empty bureaucratic hurdle for getting financial assistance.

Additional Resources for Training

The offer to provide training through the three standard modules described above is generally possible within the financial limitations of sustainable programs, and also provides a great opportunity for direct Christian witness. Other training resources are also available, often through other organizations that have this as their specific objective. For example, many governments provide technical training for small businesses. And other non-profit organizations may have subsidies to provide training, especially to help the poor. They also may have written training materials and guides that would be very helpful. The problem is, in many cases, that people do not know how to access these programs. So another part of the three pre-scribed training modules is to identify and promote additional training through providing information and networking services with other organizations.

Chapter 10

Sustainable Micro-Finance Programs

The sustainability of the client projects, businesses that generate a profit, is the key to any sustainable financing program. When the concept of sustainable programs is considered, it is also important to recognize that there are substantial differences between country environments, and within a country, between different sectors of the economy. For example, as we consider the requirements for collecting revolving loan funds, even the laws related to loan collections differ from one country to another. It is not possible to design a "cookie cutter" approach that is applicable to all situations. Even the style and format of application forms will vary greatly from one place to another.

There are principles, however, that do not vary. Basic questions to determine the viability of a business will be necessary in all cases. Some form of record keeping for clients is needed, and all the programs need to define administrative procedures and reporting systems. The capacity of the organization to present reports for the board of directors, and for other publics, is a key requirement for accessing additional funds from other sources, as well as for operational viability.

The Project Supervisor

This viability evolves over time. The program begins with volunteer personnel, then full-time staff often drawn from the church and working, at the beginning, as field staff with oversight of client projects. The performance of the project supervisors is critical to the success of the organization, because they are the ones who really know the clients and their businesses. Even with all of the analysis, it is often the personal contact that is critical in approving proposals for funding, especially in determining the credibility of the information presented. The number of clients and projects that each supervisor can handle on a monthly basis is also the most important single cost factor that impacts overall program financial sustainability.

The project supervisor not only helps to analyze proposals, but is also the key person providing follow-up after financing a project. He/she is the key person implementing the concepts provided in the training, as well as the source of information for how the project is going. In the case of community banks, the project supervisor is the staff person who attends the meetings and who knows all of the members.

The tasks of the project supervisors should be defined in relation to the number of clients, field projects, or amount of capital they are supervising, and this "load per staff person" is used to analyze the targets necessary for financial self-sufficiency. Again, this will vary greatly from one place to another, due not only to different salary ranges, but also to the conditions for providing oversight for projects. For example, if a person can be assigned to a relatively small geographical area, they can visit many more projects than if there were great distances between them. As the program grows, if there is a graduation process from small to bigger loans, supervisory needs may decline even as amounts provided grow larger, because the clients are already known. Programs that allow repeat loans also may not require an investment in training for the repeat clients. Volunteer assistance with consulting on small projects can reduce costs, and the decentralized mutual assistance expected of community banks and solidarity groups allow these to be considered, from a supervisory perspective, as one "client," because generally only one visit is required to meet with the entire group.

It would be great to find project supervisors that can evaluate projects, provide meaningful consulting assistance, and also help with training. However, it is not always possible to find such people, especially at the salary levels that are proposed to get the program started. The most important characteristic of potential staff people is to be willing and interested in getting out with the projects, rather than wanting to be behind a desk. Perhaps the best assistance for entrepreneurs comes from staff that have an entrepreneurial interest themselves, who have either had businesses, or have plans to start their own businesses.

As the hands and feet of the organization, it is also important that staff have a Christian commitment. They are also required to do a certain amount of office work, and in many cases get involved in transfers of funds, either to finance projects or collect capital, interest, or fees. So they must be people with integrity.

Once the program grows, usually one of the more experienced supervisors is assigned to supervise the work of the others. Though additional staff may also be needed for office and accounting tasks, the type of person involved in field supervision may not qualify for these roles. This is where leadership of the board may be required to define job descriptions and assist in a growth process where people from outside the agency may be needed to confront growing administrative complexities. This has proved traumatic in some cases, even for the church, when professionals that were neither part of the founding of the project, nor part of the church congregation, are brought in to supervise those who were founders, and who are part of the church. The administrative requirements of the program have to take precedence over career path expectations of staff. At the same time, consideration must be given to salary scales and incentives that motivate good staff people to stay in the organization.

Field staff must understand that the success of the entire program depends on the viability of the productive economic activity they are supervising, especially because the poor have no resources to pay back capital except those generated from their successful businesses. So the process of evaluating their capacity to set up a viable enterprise, through the application, review, and training phase that the project supervisor is so involved with, is critical, along with proper investment of funds and timely assistance through field visits. The work of the project supervisor is critical to the success of the program.

The performance of field staff can be evaluated through the quantitative data of the client under their supervision such as payment records and participation in training or consulting events. Since the assigned client load may exhibit results that cannot all be impacted by the supervisor, the evaluation should also include other measurement tools. A short form used for all supervisory visits should be filled out with a description of what was addressed, and signed by the client. This also documents that projects were visited, and promotes that the visit be more than a formality, requiring the identification and addressing of problems in the business, and an inquiry into the personal development of the client and his/her family.

The form also can be filed with the project information, and will allow a better understanding of what happened, in case the business develops problems in the future. The brief report on visits should be reviewed by program management, and used as a planning tool. The project supervisors are responsible for a defined portfolio, but give special attention to cases where clients are having difficulty, or where payments are not being made on a timely basis. The monthly payment records combined with the narrative on project visits provide a basis for planning future activity. A visit to a client where everything is going very well may take only 15 minutes, whereas a visit to a problem project may require several hours. The form used for supervisor visits allows management to understand how the project supervisors are organizing their time to promote successful projects in the portfolio under their control.

Reporting on the Payments of Capital and Interest

It is critical that timely information be available for project supervisors and management on client payments. The ability to generate this information is a critical indicator of whether the organization that has begun an economic development program has the capacity to succeed. Many donors to economic programs will provide a small amount of seed capital, and request a copy of the monthly accounts receivable reports before they disburse additional funding. Without a record of client payments, it is not possible to promote sustainable recycling of the financial resources.

The funds for establishing a business incubator, for initial loan capital of a community bank, or for solidarity or individual loans are disbursed by the organization only after establishing a written payment plan that clients have agreed to. For business incubators, the plan often is based on a percentage of monthly revenue; for community banks it is a payment on the externally funded group loan, and for solidarity and individual loans it is an amount per person. In some cases a local bank account is used as a collection mechanism, to minimize the need to handle cash, and reporting on payments is done either by presenting a copy of the bank deposit, or from information that the bank presents to the organization. Whatever mechanism is used, a monthly report must be derived from the process that allows project supervisors to know that all clients are keeping their payment commitments.

The preparation of these financial reports is complex due to the multitude of small payments, and the need to calculate for the payment of capital and a service fee, usually collected through an interest percentage. If clients do not pay on time, the interest fee may be different from the one initially contemplated in their payment plan. Funds received have to be divided between capital, interest, service fees, and any penalty for late payment. There are many accounting programs that can help to keep all of this in order, because once an organization has more than 50 clients, it is very difficult to manage detailed payment schedules and revised collection information by hand. Furthermore, the analysis of client payments impacts on funds available to pay organizational expenses, and the provision of capital to new projects.

The Importance of Collecting Capital and Fees

The concept of promoting economic development through specialized organizations is based on the hypothesis that it is possible to recycle capital to new clients, and at the same time collect interest or fees sufficient to sustain operations. If capital is not paid back, there will be no funds to recycle. If interest or other fees are not paid, subsidies will be required to keep the project going. Unless collections are made, the funds will be lost, and the organization will quickly disappear.

Even if subsidies become available to support the project when payments are not made, this has a very negative impact on the image of the organization. First of all, it is ironic that projects for businesses that supposedly generate profits would have to be supported by donations. Secondly, as clients with a defined payment plan are not held responsible for those payments, news of this circulates in the community, and the organization suffers a psychological vulnerability with all of its clients, in that the image is created that it is not really necessary to pay, and to keep commitments. In many developing countries the lack of integrity in financing of projects with the poor is considered a major liability, as governments and international institutions, by not enforcing payment commitments, have taught people that they do not really have to keep commitments. Teaching people that they do need to have integrity is one of the aspects of ministry of economic development programs.

In fact, the disbursement of capital without sufficient attention to the requirement to pay back the funds is irresponsible and damaging. The public sector "loan programs" in Latin America in the 1980s generated a popular saying, " he is a greater fool who pays a loan than the one who gives it." Through a variety of undisciplined financing schemes, the poor have been taught, in some places, that there are no consequences if they do not keep commitments. In some cases the perception of "economic development" is nothing more than the expectation of a donation, with the image created that these are resources that people are entitled to, without any reference to paying them back. The sad thing about this phenomenon is not only the difficulty it creates for organizations whose very existence depends on collecting capital and fees, but also that the track record of programs with the poor eliminates incentives to provide them financial services.

This issue also raises the importance of sustainable and viable client projects. If the person or group that is obtaining an injection of capital for a defined business project is only considering this as a transfer of donated funds they deserve, the program is in trouble. And if the project that is funded has to be liquidated to pay back the capital, or must take new capital from high interest loan sharks to survive, even timely payment of capital cannot be considered a sign of success. It is well known that many business projects in the informal sector funded by organizations, which provide capital to help the poor, leave their clients worse off than before, with a business failure and a large debt to pay. These are often loans of desperation, rather than loans of hope for a better future.

An organization set up to promote economic development must be capable of collecting funds based on successful client projects. It is understandable and expected that there will be some cases where clients pay late, or are not able to pay, but in every case a serious commitment to promote payments will be made. The impact of the provision of financial resources will complement other subsidized social programs, but will not become, through lack of collection discipline, a subsidized program. It is understood from the beginning that the expectation that clients will keep their commitment to pay is serious.

Key Elements in the Promotion of Payments

The critical issue for on-time payments is the viability of the economic activity that was funded. If the business is not profitable, payments must be generated by other sources, and poor people have few other resources. Again, the initial evaluation of the business proposal is important, as is the training and technical assistance provided in the initial phases of business installation.

Even if the business is profitable, poor administration or an increase in consumption patterns can consume all of the net profits before funds are set aside for payments. The evaluation of the administration of the business is one of the specific goals of field visits. Financial review would include an analysis of how profits are being handled, identifying personal use of funds, reinvestment in the business, and what is being set aside for payments. One goal is to increase the income of the people involved in the projects, but salaries should be defined in advance so that limits are set. Primary attention should be given to the payment plan.

This plan should be well defined in advance, and this is one of the most important aspects of the system for collection of funds. When the program is first presented to potential clients during the first training session, the concept of the importance of the payment plan should be emphasized, and an explanation made about why it is important. The training sessions also include not only the listing of the projected payments, but also the formulas for how the list is generated. The expectation of monthly payments is presented, as well as the penalties assessed for late payment.

When funds are disbursed, the documentation clearly presents a listing of the payments, and also specifies what happens when payments are not made. Clients are provided a receipt for each payment, which also specifies the date of the next payment, or is checked off against a listing of payments that the client has. The monthly reporting for project supervisors also contains the client payment histories, and clients are reminded of payment requirements during the supervisory visit. The steps by the organization to confront late payments are well defined in advance, and are put into operation when clients fall in arrears.

Incentives for Promoting On-Time Payments

The definition of procedures for late payments is preceded by a discussion of reasons why people may want to pay on time. In general, late payments are assessed some type of additional penalty, but this may not be sufficient to impact client behavior. For business incubators, a significant part of the evaluation of whether the employees can handle the business as owners is their capacity to make payments. For community banks, in the case that payment of the external loan is not provided in a timely manner, some access to the group savings pool is often invoked.

For solidarity and personal loans, an added incentive is the approval for subsequent and larger loans. These are conditional on maintaining a good payment record. Many clients have a vision for expanding their businesses through successive stages of growth, expecting additional outside capital to do so. If they understand that such assistance is dependent on their demonstration of keeping payment commitments, this provides them with a strong motivation to keep their payment schedule, or even in some cases to pay in advance.

Clients who pay late also receive special attention of the project supervisors, and may be motivated by these staff people to get their payments in order. The pressure brought on them by project supervisors is due, in part; to the fact that these program employees are evaluated on the basis of how well their projects succeed. Chronic late payments result not only in a focus on the particular business, but in what might have been at fault in the initial program analysis, the client selection process, or past supervisory visits by program staff.

The Policies for Accounts in Arrears

The accounting system will provide a monthly reporting of client accounts, and each project supervisor will receive the listing for his particular portfolio. As field visits are planned, the clients with late payments will receive priority, and written visit reports will include response to the question of why the particular project is not paying on time.

If the payment is late due to issues over which the client has not control, like the weather, natural disasters, political events, sickness, etc., the client is often granted a reprieve from any type of penalty, and allowed to get back on schedule in the months that follow. In the case of serious crisis situations, such as death of one of the project principals, an entire new schedule of payments may be developed. There are often cases where it is not possible, however, to determine if external factors really are the cause, and in these situations the exemption from penalties is for a short period of time, and also should be subject to management approval.

If the payment is late due to natural business cycles, difficulty in collections of outstanding accounts, special problems with production, etc., then help will be provided to address the specific need. Penalty fees will be charged, but the basis for the payment problems will be noted in the client files with the expectation that the project will soon return to its anticipated patterns.

There may be very special cases where natural or personal disasters or other destructive events outside of the control of the client make it impossible for the business to continue. These cases should be considered part of the anticipated losses that might be expected, and on an accounting basis should be declared as uncollectable. However, such a declaration should not only require management approval, but also the approval of the board of directors.

If the payment is late due to irresponsibility of the client, or if the evaluation of the late payment demonstrates that the business has no possibility of being viable, efforts should be made to collect the capital by an immediate liquidation of the project assets. This may be required during the first months of operation, when the initial capital has been used and the "honeymoon" is over.

It is common that clients might keep some of the initial loan and use it to pay the first few quotas. The true cash flow of their productive activity is obscured by this, and cannot be determined until the loan amount is used up. If the cash flow is insufficient to sustain the business and provide for payments, it is better to address this as quickly as possible, both for the good of the organization and for the client.

The temptation simply to refinance projects by changing the paperwork that defines payment should be avoided. Though this appears to help the organization by defining away their accounts in arrears, the underlying problems of the businesses that are not paying on time still exist. Management of micro finance programs must be willing to face reality, as they do not have access to donated funds to use to hide non-performing projects. Social development projects, it is said, "have no memory," as they are funded by grants and not required to demonstrate viability. Economic development projects do have a memory, and problems with funded projects cannot be hidden simply by redefining accounts receivables on paper.

Payment plans generally separate out the amount of capital being paid from fees and interest amounts. This distinction is relevant to the client, because it enables him to see how much the service charges are. It is important in the case of business incubators, because the potential owners can evaluate how the rental fee they are paying as employees might be converted to paying for the business, were it their own. In the case of late or partial payment, fees and interest are always paid before any of the amount is applied to capital.

The separation of the payment is more important to the organization, because the fees and interest are the basis of its financial sustainability. The payment of these amounts is generally recorded on a cash basis, rather than on an accrual basis, recognizing both the risk in obtaining this portion of the accounts receivables, and the importance of collection for the organization's budget. Posting of interest receivables as income, before the amounts are paid, can result in theoretical income that cannot be used to pay real expenses. The costs of the organization, and specifically the salaries of the staff, depend on the actual collection of interest and fees.

Payments are considered in arrears the first day after payment is due, but since client reports are usually provided monthly, by the time the project supervisor finds out about the late payments they may already be many weeks behind. The process of visits to determine the background for late payments is therefore very important, with the goal of visiting first all of those clients who appear on the arrears list. In the case that the visit results in a definition for getting back on their defined payment plan with special payments to make up for the late payment, this should be presented in a signed written document and included in their file.

If commitments made during this visit are not kept, and the account continues in arrears, the program director should send a formal letter to the client or group requesting that accounts be put in order within three business days, or the organization will take measures to collect capital. This letter should remind the client of their initial commitment and any revisions defined through supervisory visits. It should also define the measures to be taken: for business incubators, the assets will be taken, for community banks, the savings pool will be charged, for solidarity loans the other members of the group will be asked to make payment, and for individual loans the cosigners will be notified of collateral taken. Variations in these measures may exist depending on the particular context of the program, but an official letter, on organization stationery, with reminders of specific actions to be taken, has proven to be a very good mechanism for promoting collections.

The absence of any response to this letter probably means that more than 60 days have already transpired since the payment was due. The client should be encouraged to pay any amount they can, and at least to cover interest and fees. However, if there is no response, the case should be presented to management, and perhaps to the board credit committee, for legal collection. By this time the case will be evident in the organization's financial statements, and a brief report from the project supervisor should be circulated to recommend specific actions.

The handling of the case should be determined after consultation, and organization management or board members may be willing to try their hand at getting a response, especially if the clients are related to the church in some way.

If management or the board decides to contract a lawyer, the legal collection process also begins with a letter that notifies the client of the need to pay the entire loan. In some cases this letter alone is sufficient to get the client back on track. However, if this does not happen, the legal collection process should be implemented.

This is not because used equipment is valuable, nor is it anticipated that cosigners or other collateral can be easily converted into payments. The fees that lawyers charge also consume a major portion of any amount that is collected through the legal process. What motivates a professional effort to promote collection after 120 days or more of arrears is the fact that the entire image of the program is under observation. If defined procedures for collecting funds are not implemented, the organization will create an image that it is really not serious about needing funds to be paid back, and many other clients, and potential clients, will plan also not to pay their loans, finding other more important uses for their funds. Irresponsible clients who do not pay will destroy the entire credibility of the program, as the news that one client was able to get away with this without problems will quickly spread to the entire client population.

The need to take a strong position on collections is one of the reasons presented for separating the program from the church, as sometimes the people who believe they do not need to pay have acquired this belief, somehow, through their church association. The sad irony is that economic development programs have played a special prophetic role in identifying that some established church members, and even pastors, do not practice integrity in the business environment. If this person has a loan and does not want to pay, the economic development program has the special "ministry" of demonstrating that Christians also need to be held accountable.

The very serious nature of a legal collection process also calls for management evaluation of how the situation was allowed to happen. Can evidence of the problem be identified in the initial application? Did the supervisor do sufficient evaluation of the project? Was the training adequate? Were there any warning signs in the field visit reports? It is often the case that one or two people test a newly started economic development organization by simply deciding not to pay, and it may be that the problem situations encountered are part of the learning curve. It is important to make sure that all of the lessons were learned from what was experienced.

Recycling of Sustainable Financial Assistance for the Poor

One reason that the concept of sustainable financing is proposed is that subsidies for projects are getting harder and harder to obtain, and programs that depend on donations can only help a few people and then they are depleted. The advantage of a project that is able to recycle funds over and over for new clients is not only that it is easier to market to donors, but also that it creates a sustainable foundation for helping many people over a long period of time, independent of subsidies. Even if the local church discontinues any involvement in the economic project, it should be able to continue on its own without external support.

The fact that these programs can be economically self-reliant does not mean that subsidies are bad in themselves, just that they are frequently difficult to obtain. The methodology of recycling capital in a sustainable manner is attractive in many situations where there are relatively few resources, and if subsidies do become available to support specific aspects of the program, such as the technical training components, they can be well utilized for short periods of time without impacting the financial foundations of the entire program.

There are three levels in understanding the cost components of economic development programs in relation to financial sustainability:

1- The most basic level, and easiest to understand, is the level of total direct costs, including placement of capital, training, supervision, collection, and general administration. These must be covered by the fees and interest generated by the program, or they will begin to consume the capital that the program has available for funding businesses.

2- The second level of costs would also include a reserve amount for uncollectable loans, a bad debt reserve fund. The amount that should be put into a reserve depends on the loan performance, but given the fact that lending to the poor is inherently risky, at least 5% of the total amount of outstanding capital should be covered by such a reserve. When specific projects go into the legal collection process, the total loan balance of these projects can be written off against this reserve amount. It is important to note that funds written off can still be collected, but should be registered off of the official book-keeping, and reported as special revenue if repaid.

3- The third component of costs, and a major issue in developing countries, is an amount to offset inflation and devaluation. In many cases there is a continuing decline in the value of the dollar in relation to local currency, and unless this is covered through interest and fees, it will result in a loss of value of the capital fund. The margin to cover this amount must not only be generated, but also continually capitalized, i.e. added to the loan fund balance.

The goals of the economic development organization should include a financial sustainability that includes these three levels of costs. This will not happen immediately, as a subsidy will be necessary to place the initial capital, and revenues will increase over time, as the funds are placed and the project grows. It often takes three years from the time of organizational start-up to program financial sustainability. Monthly financial reports should clearly demonstrate the progress in relation to this goal, and an analysis of direct costs, uncollectable accounts, and inflation/devaluation should be reviewed periodically in setting fees and interest definitions. Though organizations are not expected to become financially sustainable immediately, progress towards that goal is a major factor in obtaining the additional capital from donors, and without additional capital it becomes more difficult to progress towards financial sustainability.

Progress Towards Financial Sustainability

When the church starts the program, it often begins operating out of the church facility, with volunteer staff. The first tasks are the definition and design of the program. The first expenses are usually related to an initial staff person and their costs, plus all of the legal and paperwork costs of getting the organization off the ground. Monies coming into the program from outside donors will probably be almost entirely for the capital fund for projects, with very little used for the program.

As the project grows, new personnel may be hired, sometimes a director who may oversee the work of the initial staff person, and be assigned further development of the project. At this stage a separate office is often set up, which helps in promoting a separate identity and also in clearly distinguishing the costs from church-related costs. The program begins to accumulate its own furniture and equipment. It starts to have an identity of its own, and funds obtained from donors may not only be used for the loan fund, but to build a basic infrastructure for support of the program-furniture, computers, vehicles, and other equipment. At this point the project probably needs to be subsidized, with careful attention to patterns of spending in relation to revenue.

Once the project reaches a mature level, it can demonstrate that it is able to cover all of its costs from revenues, even after assigning an amount for a reserve for bad debts, and capitalizing an amount of funds equal to the devaluation/inflation rate. It should be noted that devaluation is generally used as a proxy for the inflation rate due to the political factors involved in defining inflation, and the fact that funds are often sourced in dollars, so the goal of maintaining their value in dollars creates an understandable benchmark.

The mature economic development organization promotes sustainable economic activity, and is at the same time sustainable from fees and interest that it charges for its own services. It has an independent administration from the church, though connected through board members who are from the church, and by objectives that include Christian witness, being implemented by Christian employees.

Chapter 11

Common Principles for Success in Business Enterprise

The success of whatever productive economic activity we propose should first be predicated on an analysis of the environment in which we find ourselves. We need to ask the question of how our business impacts society. It appears, for example, that the free market economics and globalization that has been promoted at the start of the 21st Century is having little positive impact in developing countries. We need to find models that are consistent with the Gospel, and that really can help people. The accepted concept of industrial production, with man as an economic factor with seemingly no intrinsic value, is not founded on Christian principles. So we would look for an alternative understanding, where in our concept of the business:

- We recognize that the life of the community also includes the physical environment, flora, fauna, and natural resources.

- We recognize the capacity of people to create and maintain their style of life, their music, their traditions, and their culture.
- We recognize the difference between real needs and created needs.
- We recognize that quality of life is not what we see presented on television or in our teen culture, and cannot be measured based on what we own or what we are able to consume.
- We recognize that we have to open ourselves to the Holy Spirit to find new ways to do our work, listening to those around us, delegating authority, and promoting more flexibility and creativity.

Our expectation is to see the values of the Kingdom of God in the daily administration of the business, integrated in some way with the outreach of the church.

As we call on God to help us make wealth, to begin programs to promote productive economic activity as a ministry strategy, we acknowledge that the creativity we need for the 21st Century is a big prayer item. The poor continue to get poorer, in spite of all the major technological improvements. The promotion of international trade appears to have lowered employment levels in many places. The marketplace has become increasingly competitive.

What a time for Christians to take a leadership role in promoting productive economic activity! Whereas managers in multinational companies focus on the marketplace of the middle and upper classes, perhaps Christians can begin to focus on successful business models for the 4 billion poor that are at the bottom of the pyramid, with less than $1,500 income per year. Whereas governments have defined incentives for big companies, perhaps

Christians can promote a better understanding of how small-scale operations can develop world scale capabilities. What are the best businesses for the rural villages and shantytowns in the 21st Century? How can a business make profits in markets that appear to be unorganized, local, and limited?

There are some important variables that impact on the success of the economic projects:

- Source of the business idea: With credit programs, the concept of the economic activity comes from the person requesting the loan. In the other models presented, it comes from leadership in the church, the initial organizing committee, and other sources. The key question in this economically competitive environment in which we operate is how to identify what business is profitable.

The input of the program director and staff is critically important in defining and evaluating the business concepts for micro enterprise programs. Advice from the board, from Christian professionals, and even from donors may be significant in defining the business plans for other projects. For example, in the case of Granja Roblealto, the chicken farm that supports a children's ministry in Costa Rica, the idea of the business came from the principal donor, as it was a highly technical business that he knew in the U.S. environment.

- Source of the financing: Although some of the funds may be sourced locally, in many cases the implementation of economic development requires outside funding. Donors therefore may also play a role in project design. The development of contacts for funding and the presentation of proposals become important elements in the success of the project.

When churches begin programs in economic ministry, they often start by pooling money from within the congregation, to help members of the congregation, or for specific needy populations such as ex-prisoners, alcoholics, or other rehabilitated people. The access to funding of this nature is dependent on demonstrating that people in the church or the needy population are being helped. The easiest way to obtain external funding for economic ministry is through micro credit proposals, because donors are promised that once the program is capitalized, it can run on a sustainable basis without further requirements of subsidy. Endowment and mission business funding generally comes from people committed to the underlying ministry, and the specific business concept, in these cases, is not so important. Service enterprises that cover their costs generally evolve from subsidized ministry, and as donations decline have access only to local, self-generated funding. For example, the network of elementary schools started and operated by the Blaz de Leso church in Northern Colombia are partially supported by local government funding, which will need to be replaced over time by user fees.

- Definition of who owns the project: Except for the case of loans, the assumption has been that the economic development projects are owned and supervised by non-profit boards, with church leadership involvement. This is a fundamental issue, and must be well defined prior to project initiation. Note that, in the case of loans, the ownership of the project by the loan principal is critical in assuring payback. But even in that case, the managers of the loan program will be able to influence the loan principal, especially with regards to promoting a successful project.

When there are problems, a definition of authority is necessary to address the problem issues. The nature of the business environment is that unresolved problems will simply self-destruct the project. On the other hand, when there is success, it must also be clear how benefits will be distributed. For example, in missionary support businesses it is very critical to define who will be supported with net revenues, and at what level.

- Management and supervision: The church and the board of the project delegate this role to full-time professionals, because after the initial organization they do not have time to provide adequate oversight. It becomes very important, then, to define who is responsible for the management of the project, and to find the right people for this.

The management of economic ministry is the most critical factor in the success of these programs, and especially the entrepreneurial orientation of management. It is not easy to find good managers of integrity willing to work with the level of staffing, and relative lack of funding that is available for economic ministry. The key is that they catch a vision for business as a ministry tool, and see that it is much more than a job. It should perhaps be noted that, in all cases presented in this book, those involved in the oversight of the projects could be making far more money, with much greater professional prestige and "career path" potential, at other jobs in the secular arena. But they have chosen to work in economic ministry as a Christian vocation.

- Definition of markets: Even with the loans, it is always necessary to ask about market assumptions, as this is one of the key factors in the success of the business. In the other methodologies it is also of first importance to define and understand the market for products or services. This is an area where innovation is needed, especially in the informal sector.

The motivation to promote business activity as a ministry liberates managers of these programs from traditional thinking about market size and market share based on commercial rates of return. Service enterprises may accept a simple break-even instead of having to make money, and this frees them to focus on markets of little interest to commercial enterprises. The ministry focus of church-based economic promotion allows freedom to take risks in crafting new businesses for markets with the poorer population, that may not be of interest in the existing business environment. The Christian nature of the programs also continually renews a focus on doing good for others, and defining products and services that fill gaps, help, are constructive, and are needed. For example, the Youth for Christ computer training center in Lima, Peru, is designed to help youth learn basic skills that help them get employed, while at the same time generating sufficient revenue to cover costs, and serving as a context for evangelism and discipleship.

- Appropriate and innovative small-scale technologies that are labor intensive: there are many commercial environments where special market niches can be identified based on special products for defined consumers. The production technologies required to fill these niches can be applied on a small scale, and also involve people more than machinery.

This is an area where economic ministry can excel, especially because there is relatively little competition from other sources. Big companies want large-scale technology that is capital intensive. Many Christian economic ministries have been successful at the other extreme, with small-scale technologies that are labor intensive. For example, a group of Mexicans is producing ceramics in an African country, and teaching a small-scale technology from Mexico to the local population, to improve the quality of national production. The same concept is at the foundation of the success of tent-making enterprises with solar energy in Libya and an ethnic food restaurant in Romania.

- Product distribution: It is generally assumed that the distribution networks have to be confined to existing ones in the marketplace. But again, this is a key area for innovation, and the need to create low cost, high quality alternative systems for the poor. In many cases the church, in association with other networks on both a national and international basis, could begin to promote new distribution systems to enable people to increase margins for producers, and lower prices for consumers.

The creation of local networks has been the key factor in the success of many micro credit projects, and is a major factor with the marketing of products from business incubators. A pioneer area is international marketing. For example, a Christian company in Canada has focused on a very needy area of Colombia, and has built a profitable export program that enables rural farmers to obtain higher prices for their product.

- Connection with Christian ministry: The minimum expectation is that projects will include direct Christian witness, but in some cases the connection with the

Kingdom of God could include other aspects, such as support for Christian ministry, a source of support for the church, increased tithes, and a greater participation of Christian professionals in ministry outreach.

There are also cases where economic ministry serves as the main outreach mechanism of the church. For example, in the Dominican Republic a church located in the slums of Santo Domingo sponsored a program in the neighborhood to help women increase their income. Over half of the 60 initial respondents to the advertising became Christians through their involvement in a micro credit program operating in the church.

The assumption of this book is that all of the efforts to promote economic activity will be centered in a spiritual purpose, and that commercial activity is not an end in itself, but a means. Of course, it is clear that business must make money, or it cannot survive, much less serve the church. But the purpose is not to make profits, but rather to serve.

Chapter 12

Christian Witness
for Economic Programs
as Ministry

The central purpose of international ministry is to communicate the Good News in terms that people will be able to understand, and respond to. This communication requires an integration of words and deeds, verbal concepts articulated in acts of service. This is a very exciting, serious, and worthy goal. The change in people's lives through a relationship with God through what Jesus did on the cross is actually spectacular!

Most people in this world today do not yet understand that faith in Jesus, and what He did on the cross, rescues them from the consequences of sin and results in the security of life after death with God. They also do not understand that faith in Christ makes sense out of the present, and provides meaning to life. They have not been introduced to the family of God in the local church. They really need to hear the good news, and want to.

Economic development projects provide a context in

which the Kingdom message can be presented in a holistic manner, embracing the needs of the full person, just as it was in the first church outreach. It is interesting to note that in the short letter of Paul to Titus, he mentions eight times the idea of "doing good." The Christians were known for how they reached out to help others in need, "a people eager to do what is good," (Titus 2:14) and instructed to "learn to devote themselves to doing what is good, in order that they may provide for daily necessities and not live unproductive lives..." (Titus 3:14) In a world where poverty and unemployment is increasing for the majority in the world, and where opportunities to "do good" abound, the presentation of the Good News of the Kingdom that embraces the whole person, not just the spiritual/future but also the physical/present, is very easy to talk about, and something people are anxious to hear about and see. Church outreach integrated with projects to promote education, job creation, health, and other projects that help people, seem so much more exciting and credible than entertainment and events that churches often use to attract people: elaborate music/multimedia presentations, special trips for the youth group, etc.

Even so, the presentation of the Good News seems to disappear quickly from holistic ministry projects that attempt to integrate good works and social transformation with evangelism and discipleship. One reason for this is that many Christians may not fully understand that they have specific and clear instructions to share the Good News. As Christians we exercise the gifts that we have for the glory of God, and we also share our faith story. We promote that our friends and neighbors have opportunity to participate in the family of God in the local church, and are involved in its outreach to the community. The life of the Christian should generate the question, "why do you live like that?" providing opportunity to share the "why" they do good and the "why" they do not do evil.

If we simply put these two concepts together: (1) people need to hear the Good News + (2) we, as Christians, need to share the Good News, it would seem that it would be easy to keep a vision for the expression of faith both in word and deed. So many people have never really heard the Good News, and holistic ministry is such a great means of loving others by serving, and thereby giving glory to God.

But Christians have forgotten that the message of the cross is Good News.

In North America we celebrate openness to diversity, and this is quite right in relation to race, cultural expression, language, etc. But when we accept, consciously or unconsciously, the equal validity of all religions, or the commonly stated idea that 'all faiths lead to the same truth,' we forget that the Gospel is uniquely good news. It may seem divisive to state that Jesus "is the way, the truth, and the life," but this is the Good News. God wants every person to be saved, and come to enjoy the new life in Christ. Salvation is through Christ alone. To receive God's grace and participate in His reign in this world is life changing.

If we believe this, and are also aware that more than 70% of the population of the world today define themselves as non-Christian, and even part of the remaining 30% supposedly "Christian" truly have not heard the Good News in a way that is understandable to them, there is a BIG opportunity out there for sharing the Gospel! This might motivate us to make the presentation of how to have a relationship with God a central part of our program... but we would first have to believe that the Gospel was Good News for ourselves and for others. Many no longer believe that it is so important for other people, not even for neighbors in the U.S., and therefore have no motivation to promote it.

The centrality of the Gospel, and "evangelism," have lost priority status in the Church in the U.S., which seems focused, in many cases, on its own growth and economic stability. The comfort of the U.S. churches is unparalleled, the quality of the music systems unmatched. There are many famous religious personalities in the church, and famous schools and speakers and programs. (If there had been Christian magazines in the first century, it is hard to imagine that pictures of the disciples would have been featured in advertisements...) Fundraisers are paid the good salaries to promote adequate budget, and success is apparent in the growth of members, budget, and endowment. Some of the growth is related to a genuine presentation of the Good News and not just attracting Christians from other churches, but it seems sometimes that the focus on presenting the Christian faith is "the benefits I get from God." Church involvement as part of the good American life contradicts the basic statements about Jesus as Lord (not heavenly employee or entertainer) and taking up our cross and following Him. The heroes of the faith were always those who took up the cross, and success may actually mean a decline in funding, being less popular, and more out-of-step with our culture, especially if it becomes "politically incorrect" to talk about faith. Participation in the Western church can result in a social club religious association, a "Christianity light" that views church membership as just another aspect of the good life.

> *Christians also confuse the Gospel message by diluting it and mixing the Good News with other baggage.*

There are sincere people who believe that, in addition to salvation through what Christ did on the cross, one must accept a prescribed list of doctrinal positions. Instead of doctrines there is, in other groups, a list of rules about how people should eat, drink, dress, and spend their time. The presentation of the Gospel comes packaged with a rulebook and a spirit of ownership of the truth, sort of a Good News + program. Such approaches create barriers to ministry by leading with divisiveness, and tend to stay inward oriented, promoting the orthodoxy of the existing members rather than new entrants into the family of God.

What is the Gospel?

The Good News is that Jesus loves me! Created in the image of God, I also can have a relationship to God, the creator, who affirms life, wants me to celebrate life, and have a quality life. Life encompasses all of life, the spiritual and the physical.

It is sad to see people reject the Christian faith because their only encounter with it is a long list of negatives. *There seems to be a problem in some circles with understanding what the Gospel is.* There are unethical ways of promoting the Gospel that give evangelism the bad name of proselytism. The willful misrepresentation of other views accompanied by a dogmatic mockery of their beliefs is not acceptable, for how can Christians present the Good News when they behave in a dishonest or manipulative manner? The caricature of the evangelist as one who is threatening hearers with fire and brimstone as they are mocked and intimidated is a significant barrier for the Gospel. Perhaps wanting to avoid this extreme, some Christian programs eliminate all spoken reference to faith. Some organizations that also call themselves Christian do not have defined programs for promoting the Good News at all, and appear to have adopted a religious pluralism position, even while calling themselves Christian.

Concern for a narrow presentation of the Good News does not mean that its presentation should be avoided altogether! At the same time, the diverse approaches of followers of Christ, in terms not only of rules but doctrines and services, should not be emphasized over the basic foundations of Jesus as Savior and Lord. When you ask those who have not heard this basic message about what they know of Christians, they too often speak of lists of rules, competing claims of tele-evangelism magic, or divisive and abstract dogmas. The Good News has to be presented in an understandable way, and that is a critical task that calls for holistic programs. These must be programs where the signs of the Kingdom do not squeeze out opportunities to introduce people to the King!

Promoting a Holistic Program, both Word and Deed

The key element in motivating economic development programs to focus on Christian outreach that includes evangelism is for workers to reflect on the Good News as the center of God's project. He wants everyone to have a chance to hear the Gospel. Program managers need to reflect on what the message is that people really need to hear, and if they cannot get excited about the Good News, this may not be their line of work. They also should consider how this message unites us with other ministries, and with God's other projects in the Church, His body.

Some of the aspects of verbal presentations of faith that may motivate other Christian outreach NOT to talk about it are critical to address in economic development programs. For example, take the issue of repentance from sin. One of the most common sources of problems in any economic project is that the funds are stolen. Recognition of the tendency of people to do wrong is built into program design; unethical practices destroy economic projects. So it is quite natural to acknowledge that we all sin, and need God's grace.

Our eternal condition is another issue that is natural to discuss with economic programs. Many projects and project principals are very successful. If we provide material and technical assistance that helps someone become wealthy, but do not share with them how they can have a relationship with God through what Christ did on the cross, we run the risk of simply helping them go to hell in style. After all, the invisible, unseen realities are more important than the visible. (II Corinthians 4:18)

Promoting Christian Values

The great advantage of promoting economic activity from a Christian perspective is that values that are central to the Christian faith are also critical to business success. In what ways do we expect economic development promoted by churches and Christian communities to be different from other programs? At the very least, we would expect to find an emphasis on Christian values in the workplace.

- If we were helping people who have been exploited to start their own businesses, we would not want them, in turn, to exploit others. We want to promote justice.
- If we believe that we are stewards or managers of God's creation, we will avoid polluting and degrading the environment, be careful to dispose of waste properly, and respect flora and fauna. We want to promote responsible oversight of the world that God made.
- If we believe in the importance of community, the projects we promote will involve participation with others, not a jealousy for technology and markets. We want to promote mutual assistance and cooperation in the workplace.
- If we believe that the invisible world is more important than the visible, we will promote that clients avoid materialism and the love of money. We know that money can buy a bed but not sleep, books but not intelligence, food but not an appetite, jewelry but not beauty, luxuries but not happiness. We wish the best for our clients, and that would be that they have a personal relationship with the God who created them, and all things.
- Confronted with a market system that often alienates the worker, we affirm that God created work with a rich vision of transforming, designing, crafting, producing and providing for others. Every form of work should promote and recognize basic human dignity.

- Confronted with the temptations of wealth, we affirm that our capacity to work and be productive are gifts of God, and should be put at God's service.
- Confronted with economic policies that impoverish people and devalue work, especially the work of poor rural peoples, we affirm that all human beings have the right to a job that allows them to live with dignity as persons created in the image of God.

Christian Witness of the Program Staff

The project supervisor providing consulting assistance to the small businesses is the key person for communicating a Christian testimony to the clients and participants in an economic development program. This is the one who visits and evaluates projects in the field, or who helps organize community banks, who is in contact with project principals monthly, and who knows personally the people who are involved in the projects. If a clear Christian testimony is desired, the first requirement is to recruit Christian employees, and then to train them in how they can best minister to the clients and others. Many very good opportunities to counsel people, not only in matters related to their business but also their personal lives, come through addressing problem situations in the small business. An effective Christian witness program is one that provides a timely response to people, and a word of counsel in their time of need, whether the issues are related to business or other matters.

Openness to a Christian witness perspective of the program has to begin with top management that not only promotes this orientation, but also provides the resources for its implementation. Too often the Christian nature of economic development programs, and social programs in general, become a well-kept secret, or only a fund-raising tool for certain markets. Some organizations claim that the provision of services for the poor is a Christian witness in itself, and no other expression of faith is necessary. Many promote Christian values at an official level, but neither recruits Christian staff, nor allow time for any type of Christian outreach. Their U.S. promotion highlights the concept of "sharing the love of Jesus" but there is no program component that actually mentions Jesus. Program outputs are measured only in material terms, and the invisible realities, or the idea of an eternal destiny, are not of interest.

In some programs there are evidences of Christian identity that are expressed through institutional requirements. It is common, for example, that meetings be opened with a prayer or a Bible reading. Or program staff may be required to attend a weekly devotional session. The problem with these activities, when they are a legalistic prescription for an institutional Christian identity, is that they often demonstrate the opposite of Christian witness. If there is no real faith commitment of the participants, the participation in these activities becomes just another hurdle for meeting program requirements, and actually an inoculation that prevents people from a true faith encounter with Christ.

As opposed to administrative systems, the maintenance of a vibrant Christian vision that is relevant to staff and clients cannot be implemented by operations manuals and procedures. Program management and board leadership must promote and conserve this vision. On a practical level, this means that Christian outreach must be part of the program. Time must be allowed for Christian ministry. The employees of the program should meet weekly for a time of prayer and Biblical reflection, and also to celebrate what God is doing in the lives of the people that are touched by the program activities. There also should be time set aside to equip and prepare staff to promote times of Biblical reflection with clients, and incorporate Christian witness in the personal counseling and formal training components of the project.

Measurement of program outputs should include the change in people's lives, as they are encouraged in their faith walk. The Christian outreach of the program should be part of management evaluation. Written materials should be developed to promote Christian witness with staff and clients in different contexts, and these should be periodically evaluated and updated.

Training Resources and Ideas

There are a great wealth and variety of lessons, stories, and examples in the Bible that can be integrated with all kinds of business experience. For example, Jesus was himself involved in several types of business activity, and many of the parables are directly related to productive economic activity.

What must be avoided in formal training is a legalistic perspective, with doctrinal or denominational rigidness that excludes people. Assistance should not be conditioned on accepting a certain faith definition, as not even Jesus did this. The presentation of Christian truth should build on what people already know, and build bridges instead of create barriers. The church is an organization comprised of people from many backgrounds, and the Gospel should be presented in a way that it can be understood from whatever social class, educational background, or financial level the person comes from.

Most economic programs require some type of formal technical training to be successful. It is appropriate that these training sessions begin with a time of Biblical reflection, and that they also offer the participants the opportunity to hear the Gospel in terms that they can understand. If program beneficiaries are helped with material assistance, but never get this opportunity to hear how they can have a personal relationship with God through what Christ did on the cross, we run the risk of helping them go to hell in style. After all, the invisible realities are more important than the visible.

Some of the basic themes that can easily be incorporated into training programs are:

Work as Part of the Plan of Creation

The Bible explains that God created the universe. According to the Genesis recounting, God worked for six days, then rested from His work. God created man in His image. Man was created to work as the manager in the world where God had placed him, and this job of being a steward of God's creation existed before sin entered the picture. So the concept of work was part of God's design of the universe; the role of humankind was, in part, to organize and oversee the world that the Divine Worker had created.

The Bible presents work as the means of God's provision for man, even after sin enters the picture, and makes work more difficult. There are many Bible verses that present this truth, but they are not often referred to in sermons heard in the church today, especially in developing countries. For example, the Apostle Paul, makes the statement in perhaps his first missionary letter, the epistle to the church in Thessalonica, that they "mind their own business and work with their hands, so that their daily life may win the respect of outsiders and they not be dependent on anyone." (I Thessalonians 4:11-12) This is presented in the context of describing, in this section of the letter, how to live to please God.

Why would this not be a good text to preach from? Imagine if half of the congregation was unemployed, and this text was read out loud. Someone might protest, and ask how this is to be put into practice. When the public sector is cutting back, and free market promotion results in capital-intensive investment that also reduces employment, how are people supposed to work with their own hands?

This is where we see the importance of this ministry: the promotion of productive economic activity. Programs that promote viable business activity help people to put into practice the Biblical instruction from I Thessalonians. Whether through the creation of service enterprises, or ministry support business, or business incubator or loans, the intent is to create permanent employment, and generate revenue that provides for daily necessities, and eliminate dependence on handouts. This is what people really want and need.

The Lausanne Covenant, a document describing the agenda for the Church in the last part of the 20th Century, presented the concept that "humanity was made in God's image, and therefore every person, regardless of race, religion, color, culture, class, sex or age has an intrinsic dignity that should be respected and served." (section #5 on

Christian Social Responsibility, 1974) Encouragement of productive economic activity is an important aspect of promoting human dignity. Helping people to provide for themselves and their families is a great service opportunity for the Church, and should be part of its mission.

It is also part of following Jesus, who also had much to say about the concept of work. In fact, when our Lord was asked to teach us to pray, he included in His model prayer the statement "give us this day our daily bread." He said this at a time before there were government social welfare projects or child sponsorship from non-profit organizations. Most certainly Jesus was not thinking of handouts when he taught us to pray, but rather a job to be able to provide for our needs. He knew that work was strategic for the provision of our daily needs, and had a lot of experience Himself in all kinds of economic activity.

The Words and Deeds of Jesus

We clearly see Jesus' understanding of productive economic activity in statements and involvement in some of the key industries of his time:

Fishing: Jesus loved the beach and the sea, and is often found teaching and preaching next to water. He recruits fishermen, and also appears to know and enjoy fishing. For example, in Luke 5:1-7 he tells his friends to "let down your nets for a catch."

Note that in this case Jesus, perhaps looking for a little adventure, is in the boat himself. When the results of a surprisingly big catch strain the nets, where is Jesus? He is helping to pull in the fishing nets along with the others. He is working alongside the fishermen. Later he uses the picture of the fisherman and his work to present spiritual truths, but in the background it is clear that he understood the fishing business, and liked to associate with people who worked in this business.

Agriculture: Modern textbooks on agricultural production present four basic outcomes of seed germination that are similar, in many ways, to the four cases that Jesus presents in a talk recorded in the Gospel records. If the outcomes of Mathew 13:3-8 are considered, we have (1) insufficient soil preparation for seed to take root, (2) inadequate depth of soil for seedling to mature, (3) competitive growth of other organic production preventing proper growth, and (4) adequate conditions for satisfactory production. Jesus is using his analysis of agricultural processes as the basis for presentation of spiritual truths, but in the process also demonstrates an understanding of basic farming. Perhaps lessons like this have become irrelevant in the United States, but in developing countries, the *campesino* rural farmer who hears this passage for the first time will often be extremely impressed to see that Jesus understands his world of work.

Small animal husbandry: The same phenomenon, of surprise at how much Jesus knew about a particular line of business, is even truer in relation to the production of sheep. Anyone who visits a sheep farm will be surprised by how well Jesus understood the care of sheep, as he described in John 10:1-6. Jesus understood the role of the Shepherd very well, and used this business understanding also to teach spiritual truths.

Construction: When Jesus began his public ministry at 30 years of age, announcing this in the synagogue (Mark 6.1-4), the question was, "Isn't this the carpenter?" The footnote to this passage in the New International

Version says that the statement was derogatory, meaning "is he not a common worker with hands like the rest of us?" Jesus had those hardened hands of a manual laborer, so common among both men and women in developing countries. As we have opportunity to work with such people in ministry, it is good to remember how they have hands like Jesus.

The Greek word for carpenter can include the concept of general construction, not just with wood but with other materials as well, such as stone and adobe. When Jesus says "my yoke is easy and my burden is light" in Matthew 11:30, he is using a picture perhaps drawn from his own experience of making wooden yokes, which had to match carefully the team of oxen for which they were crafted. When he states that the wise man built his house, and "dug deep and laid the foundation on rock," (Luke 6:48) he is perhaps drawing from his own experience in building houses. Indeed, the statement in Luke 14:28-29 about building a tower, but first developing a detailed plan and budget, is very much the type of statement a construction manger would make.

Some Biblical scholars believe that Jesus worked as a building contractor from his adolescence until age 30, when he perhaps turned the business over to a younger brother. We hear nothing about Joseph after Jesus was 12, and the social norm was that the oldest male child in the family be responsible for family support in the event of the death or sickness of his father. It is quite possible that Jesus managed the construction and carpentry enterprise for more than a decade, until other family members could take responsibility for family finances.

Support for this hypothesis is drawn from other substantial evidence that Jesus had direct and intense aware-ness of the administrative environment of a business:

Should an investment generate a return? Consider the parable of the talents in Luke 19. If one talent was equiv-alent to three months' salary that means that the invest-ment being considered here was more than 2 years' salary, a substantial amount. The expectation is that these resources will be put to work, and a return on investment is rewarded.

Are employees usually happy with their pay? The parable of day workers who are employed in the vine-yard, in Matthew 20, is presented for a spiritual meaning, but presents an underlying understanding of the prob-lems of personnel management. Though a just wage is paid, comparisons of compensation between workers generate resentment. This even happens in the context of church projects.

What about business ethics? The parable of the unjust administrator who knew he was going to be fired, pre-sented in Luke 16, is proof for many that Jesus knew the internal world of business. When this story is cited in client training in many developing countries, the response is, "Jesus worked in a world much like ours!" Much that happens in the world of commerce is unethi-cal, and Jesus understood this.

The evidence goes on and on. Jesus makes several statements about taxes, none particularly enthusiastic. He mentions other cases of oversight of business projects and with parables illustrates situations that seem to come from the business world. When the statement is made in Hebrews 4:15 that "we do not have a high priest who is unable to sympathize with our weaknesses, but we have one who has been tempted in every way, just as we are..." this sympathy extends also to the world of business. As we promote productive economic activity, and help people to realize the prayer that Jesus made about our daily bread, it is encouraging to know that Jesus, a small business manager himself, understands what we are trying to do.

Principles from the Ministry of the Apostle Paul

The Apostle Paul encourages Christians to follow his example, as he follows Christ. He has a great deal to teach, by word and example, about productive economic activity. It was his statement that is quoted earlier about the expectation that people work with their own hands, to provide for themselves and as a Christian testimony. In his second letter to this same church Paul is even more dogmatic about this, saying, "if someone does not work, they should not eat." (II Thessalonians 3:10) The situation is quite relevant to our day, as the church had then, as it does now, social programs to help the needy. But some were taking advantage of these programs that had no right to them, "mooching" off the church.

Paul was a leather worker, as discussed in a previous chapter. He used his work to subsidize his missionary outreach. He makes it quite clear in the first letter to the church in Corinth that he believes that the strategy of "preaching the Gospel free of charge" is better for his ministry. (I Corinthians 9:18) But he also refers to work as a basic expectation of Christians. For example, in Ephesians 4:28 he states that "he who steals should steal no more, but work with his own hands to provide for himself and also to have something to share with others in need." Again, reading this in the context of the developing world, where unemployment is common, these instructions are very difficult to heed without help from somewhere. Globalization, free markets, and the political environment of the early 21st Century seem to be making life for the poor majority worse, instead of better. The Bible says to work, but work is sometimes hard to find.

Chapter 13

The Challenge
that Lies Ahead

Promoting productive economic activity can be an effective tool for Christian ministry. But it is not easy. It is important to acknowledge this, and identify some of the significant problem issues. The saying "if they give us lemons, we need to learn to make lemonade" is appropriate for thinking about the challenges for any successful economic development program.

The "Evil Powers" Lemon

The struggle with a world dominated by greed and sin is quite notable in the world of economics. Governments craft policies to help their citizens, and in the process impoverish people of other countries. Big companies ruin smaller companies in a competitive environment with few rules and no protection. Unethical practices are common, just as they were in Jesus' time.

Christian authors write a great deal about the world economy, injustice, and unfair practices. What is missing is a concrete plan for how to live, and especially how "to work with your own hands," in the meantime. Whatever one believes about economic systems, the fact is that we confront the "lemons" of increasing poverty, gross social injustice, and awesome economic inequality. We need to pray and exert all the political capital we have to address these problems, but at the same time face reality.

It is this type of perspective that motivated the substance abuse recuperation program in Mexico to teach recovered drug addicts and alcoholics to make tortilla presses. They discovered a product that was easy to sell, that can be made from inexpensive scrap lumber, and produced with simple technologies. This productive economic activity provides for families, and a respectable and meaningful means of "working with their own hands."

The problems of the region where these people live are enormous, and due to the proximity to the U.S., many churches from the north respond by bringing down food and clothing to hand out, or with donated services for health and basic education. But what people want is the capacity to earn their daily bread, not have it donated to them, and to pay for their own local medical services. A job is valued more highly than anything else, because it is the key to the capacity to provide for everything else. Our ministry should include not only service, but listening to those we serve. If we listen, we may find that there are ways we can help people to increase income and become employed, even in the very difficult circumstances in which they find themselves.

The "Lemon" of the Church Context

The irony of many programs started for the church is that they develop to a point where they exclude church members. Working with the church is not easy, and the community that God chose to work with has always been to some extent dysfunctional. The people of Israel started complaining soon after they got their freedom from Egypt, the disciples were occasionally problematic, and Paul had all kinds of struggles with the first leaders of the church.

God uses weak and common people like you and me, instead of the smart, rich, and well-connected crowd. God does this, apparently, to show that His activity in the world comes from Him, not us. So we need to have realistic expectations. Will someone use his or her church affiliation to try to benefit from the program? That happens a lot. Will someone who appears to have integrity turn out to be irresponsible? Count on it.

The special problem for missions and Christian agencies is that they may have a tradition of providing donations, and the initial communication that an economic program is different, requiring a pay back of capital, may be traumatic. Usually someone will test the boundaries, and it will be necessary to take action. It is disappointing to realize that people considered spiritual leaders in the context of church meetings are unethical and irresponsible in the context of a business. This test of Christian commitment may be a good thing, but it is also very hard when people fail the test.

On the other hand, it is exciting to see cases where the church has benefited greatly, and expanded its ministry, through economic programs. In a small church in one of the poorest slums of Santo Domingo, the leaders decided to use the community bank concept as an evangelistic tool. They had noticed that most people in the community did not want to enter the church, having no understanding of the music or how to participate in a church service. Many thought that the church was part of a dangerous religious sect.

To promote interaction with the neighbors, an invitation was made, through distributing flyers, of a new program to be started in the church to promote income. It was called the neighborhood village bank, and the methodology was described to all of those attending a first meeting, scheduled during late morning in the church building.

From this small project a solid community bank program was begun, with involvement of those in and out of the church. Every meeting begins with a Biblical reflection, but though the pastor and leaders participate, the community group has its own board, incorporation papers, accounts, and even one part-time employee. Over a two-year period 17 people from the community have become Christians and joined the church through the program, and a few others have joined other churches. The image of the church in the community has been completely changed, and it is known for its interest in promoting development for non-members as well as members.

The Lemon of Limited Access to Resources

Once the importance of productive economic activity has been accepted, the question arises of how to fund it. Some people are used to the idea of donating money for evangelistic outreach, or even for donations of clothes, food, or medicine. Appeals for funds for these types of programs are common, but how are economic programs to be funded? The saying that "if you give a man a fish, he eats for a day, but if you teach him to fish, he eats for a lifetime" does not take into account that it is much easier to raise funds for the donated fish than for the educational and funding program involved in empowering the person to fish on his own.

One key is to help donors to understand this problem. The pictures of the starving child may be great to raise funds, because they generate an emotional response. But simply providing food does not address the real problem, that the parent has no employment. In the long run, helping the parent to get a job is cheaper than subsidizing the food, clothing and educational costs of the children. Productive economic activity is more complicated, and perhaps less picturesque, but a better solution.

Churches in developing countries are catching this vision, and pooling their own resources to promote economic development. At a meeting where the concept of economic development was being presented in Brazil, a medium-sized church presented how it had raised a revolving fund of $30,000 from church members to help increase incomes and create jobs. They never even considered presenting a proposal to external donors, but were able to start a project with their own resources.

May God give us the wisdom in the application of the tool of productive economic activity in the context in which we live today.